A Show of Hands

Using Puppets with Young Children

Ingrid M. Crepeau
and M. Ann Richards

Redleaf Press®
www.redleafpress.org
800-423-8309

Published by Redleaf Press
10 Yorkton Court
St. Paul, MN 55117
www.redleafpress.org

First edition 2003
Cover design by Laurie Ingram-Duren
Interior design by Dorie McClelland, Spring Book Design
Photos by Ingrid M. Crepeau and Michele Valeri
Printed in the United States of America

Library of Congress Cataloging-in-Publication Data
Crepeau, Ingrid M., 1948-
  A show of hands : using puppets with young children / Ingrid M.
Crepeau and M. Ann Richards.
     p. cm.
Includes bibliographical references.
  ISBN 978-1-929610-36-5
1. Puppet theater in education. I. Richards, M. Ann, 1961- II. Title.

PN1979.E4C75 2003
371.39'9 — dc21

2003012809

Printed on acid-free paper

Dedication

In memory of my mother, Olga.
I.M.C.

In memory of my father, the educator.
M.A.R.

Contents

Foreword

Puppets dominated my creative play throughout my childhood. I made my first puppet, a clown, when I was six years old. My eight-year-old big brother made a Davy Crockett puppet, and my dad hand-carved a musket and a powder horn for old Davy. My mom made beautiful costumes for both my clown and Davy but I was jealous and wished I had made a Davy Crockett puppet myself. I ended up putting on a Davy Crockett puppet show, and my clown played the role of Davy. I've been doing puppet shows ever since.

At the age of six, I was typical of most young children who I work with today. I was fanciful, sliding easily into the world of pretend, and was in touch with my imagination. While whimsical, young children are still preoperational and need something concrete as a jumping-off point: a toy, a book, a story, or a puppet. My experience has shown that puppets can provide that concrete touchstone while at the same time encouraging the child's all-important imagination.

This book grew out of years of experience with puppets and young children. Over the last thirty years, my teacher and puppeteer friends and I have collected stories about these experiences both as a way to better understand the art form in the early childhood community and as a way to affirm and support educational work with puppets. These shared stories sustained and entertained us as we experimented. As you begin to include puppets among your teaching techniques, I want you to join our puppeteer's circle and share in these stories. Many of the adventures we had in the classroom have been included in this book as sidebars to illustrate points made throughout the text.

I hope your work with puppets and young children is as rewarding, productive, and entertaining as mine has been.

Ingrid Crepeau

Acknowledgments

The authors would like to thank the following people for their assistance: Kay Blackburn, Dr. Victoria Brown, Dr. Bernardo J. Carducci, Marcia Daft, Cathy Eliot, Kathy Kolb and Redleaf Press, Janice McKelvey, Stephanie Merik and her first-grade class at Hunter's Woods Elementary, Sarah Pleydell, Stephen Simpson, Jake Simpson, Lois Taylor, and Cynthia Word.

Ingrid and Ann would also like to thank the friends and family who encouraged and supported them, as well as reading endless drafts: Chris, Ross and Grace McCarthy, Mary Richards, and Michele Valeri for all her help and for giving us the wonderful title.

CHAPTER **1**

Why Puppets?

DO YOU EVER wish you had an extra pair of hands in the classroom? Hands that could tell a gripping story, get children excited about cleanup, excite the imagination, or explain a complicated lesson on why eating apples is good? What if these extra hands were willing to work for free, never ate anything, never spoke out of turn, and were willing to sleep in a shoebox? If that all sounds too good to be true, then you haven't thought enough about bringing puppets into your classroom. This book is intended to inspire you as you explore the tantalizing world of puppets.

Educational Benefits of Puppets

Why do teachers use puppets in the classroom? First and foremost, they are exciting. Children like puppets because they add that extra touch of fun and fantasy that can make the classroom a magical place. But the ability of puppets to fascinate children goes deeper than their simple charm. Puppets can become a powerful ally for teachers because they help the students enjoy learning. With puppets, the emphasis is off the teachers' burden to impart information and is on the children wanting to learn.

In 1999 special education teacher Kay Blackburn began using puppets in the classroom. "The reaction was amazing," confides Mrs. Blackburn. "I had known that working with puppets would be fun, but I was unprepared for how effective they were. On average, the children attended longer with the puppets, and we saw developmental gains that I attribute to teaching with puppets. It has been a real revelation for everyone involved."

Mrs. Blackburn is not alone. Many teachers have found that using puppets in their classroom greatly increases their success with children. Why would this be? What makes puppets so useful and effective in the classroom? One answer comes from Dr. Lilian Katz (1993), who asks, "What do we really want the children to get out of their classroom experience?" Katz feels that the teacher's paramount goal is for the child to end up with a passion for learning, what she terms a "disposition for learning." What good is there in knowing the alphabet if it is drilled and drilled and drilled until the child wishes he didn't know it in the first place? That child will not be eager to learn anything else. On the other hand, consider a child who learns about the alphabetic principle with his puppet friend Letter Man. He looks forward to seeing Letter Man every day. Letter Man is playful and interesting and tells him what letters look like, how they sound, and how they fit into words. He wants to learn more and more about letters, sounds, and words. He is far better off than the child who learned the same information through drilling, flash cards, and recitation.

Puppets are an often-ignored key to a child's disposition to learn. If learning with puppets is exciting, then learning is exciting. And if learning is exciting, then the teacher has done her job. Puppets are naturally exciting for children and they are a marvelous tool for teachers who want to do their job well.

This book will spark your thinking about how to incorporate puppets into your classroom to benefit children's enjoyment and learning. Here are some of the reasons teachers turn to puppets:

- Puppets assist in classroom management by encouraging children's focus, providing convenient transitions, becoming an exciting reward, and by becoming tools for class control.

- Puppets can address children's many ways of knowing and learning.

- Puppets provide for learning through play.

- Puppets support developmentally appropriate practice (DAP) curriculum.

- Puppets allow the teacher to include repetition of concepts without becoming boring or redundant.

- Puppets are easily obtained or made, and can be an inexpensive addition to the classroom.

There are three charts in this chapter that provide further evidence of the powerful educational advantages that puppet use provides. The charts explore how puppet use fits with theories of play, developmentally appropriate practice, and multiple intelligences theory. With so many excellent reasons to use puppets, one might wonder why there are teachers who don't use puppets with their students at all.

Steps to Incorporating Puppets into the Classroom

Teacher attitudes regarding puppets fall into three categories. The first are those who already use puppets and want support and more ideas. Next are teachers who recognize that puppets are powerful classroom tools but are wary of using them. Finally, there are teachers who are skeptical about the use of puppets and uninterested in using them.

These skeptical teachers are unconvinced about using puppets generally for three reasons:

- Lack of experience and exposure to puppets in the classroom

- Lack of planning when using puppets in the past

- Lack of self-confidence

Ingrid: Many teachers have come up to me during workshops saying they are reluctant to use puppets. Often, it is because they have brought one into the classroom without fully planning how it will be used, and have found that the students reacted to it in an unruly manner. This experience can only leave a bad impression on the teacher. I always advise them to try again, using a quiet or shy puppet. If their use is properly thought out, puppets become a tool for classroom management, rather than an instrument that instigates classroom chaos.

All of these issues can be addressed by simple preparation. In order to begin incorporating puppets in the classroom successfully, you don't need specific skills, you don't need to be a "performer," and you don't need an excessive budget. By using the ideas in this book, anyone can include puppets in the classroom with excellent results.

Begin by identifying a goal for the classroom. It might be a specific cognitive goal, like all children learning their own phone numbers. It might be a more practical goal, like everyone willingly participating in cleanup. It might be a social goal, like practicing to wait for your turn. Or it might be a physical goal, like practicing fine motor skills. You will be limited only by your imagination.

Next, select the puppet use that would best address the goal. For example, a task puppet, Sarah the Telephone Operator, might be a good choice to help children learn their phone numbers, and a reward puppet might be used as incentive to participate in cleanup. Waiting their turn and practicing fine motor skills require involving children in the puppet manipulation. The puppet use will help determine the puppet character (person, animal, fantasy character, or inanimate object) and the puppet type (hand, rod, hat, and so on). Much more about these issues can be found in chapter 2, "Puppet Basics."

Next, design a lesson plan that introduces the puppets and sets out the rules for its use. This lesson design should be carefully thought through and include an idea of how the puppet will be revealed, what the puppet will say, and where the puppet will go when the lesson is over. This lesson should then be practiced before it's used with the children. Look in chapter 6, "Puppet Lessons," for more information about this.

Going through these steps in the simplest situations may only take a few minutes. However, some teachers may want to spend more time for more complicated lessons. The rest of this text is meant as an aide for those teachers, assisting them as they develop puppet lessons for the first time. As the material is incorporated in the classroom and the teacher becomes familiar with the concepts, the preparation time will decrease and the benefits increase. Toward these ends, this text is meant to inspire, inform, entertain, and encourage those who wish to explore the world of possibilities that puppets have to offer.

Ingrid: My friend Marcia tried using a puppet in the classroom, and she recalls the experience as frightening at worst and unbelievably distracting at best. Marcia brought Squiggy, a worm hand puppet, to introduce her circle time for the day. The children were totally taken with the puppet and when Marcia wanted to put the puppet away to continue her activities, the children were upset; they wanted to talk to the puppet worm more. Finally, Marcia compromised and put the worm down for a nap in her bag. When she pulled something else from the bag to show the children, they started chanting, "Show the worm!" and "Squiggy wants to see this!" This pattern repeated itself each time Marcia wanted to start circle time. Later she told me that it was especially frustrating because Squiggy had more influence than she did!

Marcia had begun in a very promising way. She allowed every child in the circle to touch and say hello to the puppet. Often this step is omitted for the sake of time. I find that taking the time to show each child a puppet, exciting prop, or toy helps the lesson flow smoothly. I take the puppet around the circle myself, greeting each child. This way I have more control over the situation, and can keep it moving around the circle.

What else could Marcia have done to prevent Squiggy from taking over the class? Once she had shown the puppet to her class, she put it back in her bag, effectively hiding it from the class. This can be avoided by setting the puppet on a chair or bookshelf and commenting, "Squiggy the worm will sit here and watch us play." Periodically, you can refer to the worm during the activity without even putting your hand in the puppet. Simply move the puppet when speaking for it much as a child does when having a teddy bear speak during free play.

Puppets that are requested over and over by students are powerful tools, and sometimes you need to follow the adage "if you can't beat 'em, join 'em." If a favorite puppet will help focus the children before an activity, bring it out each time to watch the lesson. Instead of working against you by distracting the children each time, it works for you by focusing them, and giving them a routine signal about what is going to happen next.

Play Theory and Puppets

George S. Morrison (1998), in his popular text, *Early Childhood Education Today,* writes of the importance of play. An examination of the eight purposes of play as described by Morrison shows that puppets support the development of all of them.

Purpose of Play	Examples of How Puppets Accomplish This
Learning concepts	A puppet asks, "What color am I?" A child must find food and feed a hungry puppet who will only eat orange objects.
Develop social skills	A teacher asks, "I want to use the red crayon, but so does my puppet Leon. What should we do?" A naughty puppet keeps interrupting and won't wait for his turn until the children explain to him why it is important to be patient.
Develop physical skills	Hand puppets give children practice with fine motor skills. A rabbit puppet explains to the children the difference between hopping and jumping.
Master life situations	A doctor puppet can expose children to the experience of a medical appointment. Through acting out a story with puppets, children are exposed to coping skills when they are away from their parents.
Practice language processes	Children provide speech for their puppets during free choice time. The teacher invites the children to help Silly Silas, a puppet with bad grammar.
Develop literacy skills	Children explore oracy and concepts about story when they put on puppet shows. Children learn about the alphabetic principle through letter-shaped puppets who make their phonemic sound when they talk.
Enhance self-esteem	Classmates applaud after a peer makes a puppet presentation. A child who otherwise may find it difficult to speak in front of a group may find pride in being able to speak for a puppet.
Prepare for adult life and roles	Students plan for a puppet presentation by making decisions about the puppets to be used, negotiating for parts, and collaborating with others in the presentation.

Developmentally Appropriate Practice and Puppets

The National Association for the Education of Young Children (NAEYC) defines developmentally appropriate practice (DAP) as educational approaches and techniques that are appropriate both to the age of the children involved and to the developmental level of the individual child (Bredekamp and Copple 1997). Puppets are a particularly effective tool in a DAP classroom as they can address the physical, emotional, social, and cognitive needs of young children.

DAP Domain	Examples of How Puppets Accomplish This
Physical needs	By using puppets, children coordinate fine motor skills in their hands with language.
Emotional needs	Puppets provide nonthreatening characters that children can question, confront, and befriend, and with whom they can identify as they work toward establishing healthy emotional relationships with people.
Social needs	Sociodramatic play with puppets allows children to try on different social roles.
Cognitive needs	Puppets provide an alternative cognitive stimulus, and are versatile enough to address almost every DAP subject teachers introduce.

Multiple Intelligences Theory and Puppets

Howard Gardner's book, *Frames of Mind* (1993), describes seven ways of "knowing," or multiple intelligences. In Gardner's subsequent book, *Intelligence Reframed* (1999), he revisits the original seven intelligences and discusses how his theory has evolved and been revised. As Gardner strives to meet the needs of a variety of children who learn in a variety of ways, we can see how puppets can easily assist a multitude of learning styles.

Area of Intelligence	Examples of How Puppets Accomplish This
Linguistic	Teachers who offer children the opportunity to speak for the puppets they are operating support linguistic learners.
	Linguistic learners may be stimulated by hearing the same thing described orally two different ways by two different puppets.
Logical-mathematical	Preschool children use this skill in deciding how many puppets and puppeteers will be needed to present a particular story.
	Children use logical-mathematical skills when measuring their hands to make puppets.
Musical	Children who have their puppets sing or dance to music are exercising their musical intelligence.
	Those who use music during a puppet show to reflect the mood of the story are using musical intelligence.
Bodily-kinesthetic	Children who design puppets using their own hands are stimulating bodily-kinesthetic learning.
	Students who use their whole bodies to perform a puppet show exercise their bodily-kinesthetic intelligence.
Spatial	As children build stages by combining existing furniture and structures, they are exercising their spatial intelligence.
	Those who make their own puppets and decide how that confined space is going to be decorated are using spatial intelligence.
Interpersonal	Children use their interpersonal intelligence as they improvise puppet scripts and conversations.
	Children who negotiate who is going to play what character must rely on interpersonal skills.
Intrapersonal	Intrapersonal intelligence is addressed each time teachers use puppets to explore feelings.
	When children respond to puppets by describing their own emotions, they are strengthening intrapersonal skills.

Ingrid: I was working in a transitional kindergarten class. All of the children were from non-English-speaking homes. Eleven different languages were represented among eighteen children. The teacher's goal was that they learn to write their names. To assist in that effort, I made up stories about the letters in their names using alphabet puppets (a stick puppet with an alphabet letter on its back representing the first initial of the puppet). One student named Vincent was born with a cleft palate. Following surgery, Vincent was reluctant to talk and use his rebuilt mouth. The adults involved thought he was very bright, and wasn't speaking because of the embarrassment he suffered when he wasn't understood. Vincent's father confided that the problem was not limited to school: his son did not speak at home either. As I performed the puppet shows for each of his classmate's names, I offered him the opportunity to participate, and he always shook his head no.

Finally the day came to do a story about Vincent's name. For the occasion, I made a Vincent the Vampire puppet. We all looked at the letters of Vincent's name, and I introduced the cast of characters: Vincent the vampire, Izzy the insect, Nettie the nightingale, Cedric the centipede, Elly the elephant, Nutty the nut (a walnut on a stick with eyes), and Tangerine Man (a plastic tangerine on a stick with a face). I performed the story for the children in storyteller style, pulling each character out of its Styrofoam stand in order for it to say its lines, then replacing it. This meant that Vincent's name was spelled out in puppets for him during the entire exercise. After I told the story, I helped the students act it out using puppets by feeding them lines as needed. I handed Vincent his vampire puppet and asked him to operate it. He took the puppet without hesitation. I prompted him,

"Vincent, make your vampire say 'This is a wonderful birthday.'" I held my breath until Vincent blurted out a beautiful and unintelligible sound. The children in the class erupted, exclaiming, "Vincent talks! Vincent talks!" For a while after that, Vincent would only speak with a vampire puppet in his hands. His teacher, his speech therapist, and even his father made a vampire puppet for him to use. A year after I left that class I bumped into Vincent's kindergarten teacher. I asked if she knew anything about Vincent. She laughed and said that Vincent had been weaned from the puppet, and had become a chatterbox!

FIG 1-1 Vincent the Vampire (simple rod puppet)

CHAPTER 2

Puppet Basics

BEFORE BRINGING A PUPPET into the classroom for the first time, the teacher should think about her goals. Some possible goals:

- Strengthen classroom management tools

- Introduce a unit using a character that can speak about the topic in the first person

- Expose children to a wider range of emergent literacy experiences

- Encourage more creative play in the classroom

- Prepare the children for an upcoming field trip

- Review a lesson, an experience, and so on

Puppets can assist in all of these goals as well as many others; however, some puppet techniques are better suited to certain goals. Puppets can be sorted and described in three different ways: by type, by use in the classroom, and by character. Thinking about puppets in these categories will help you choose the appropriate puppet for your needs.

Puppet Types

Puppets are classified by type based on how they are controlled by the puppeteer. Below we describe the six main categories of puppets and their variations. There are other styles of puppets and variations on these basic types; however, we will focus on the simplest in this text as they are the most appropriate for use with children in early childhood.

Finger Puppets

There are two types of finger puppets. One type features a glove with characters on each finger. Popular puppets in this category include birds in a nest, kittens in a basket, and characters from a story, like "Goldilocks and the Three Bears." The second type of finger puppet is worn on a single finger. While individual finger puppets are often purchased, they can easily be knit, sewn, or made by gluing felt to a cardboard tube. [FIGURE 2-1] When operating a finger puppet, the finger must wiggle or nod to indicate the puppet is speaking. Curl the other fingers down when they are not in use. If possible, use puppets on both hands to avoid awkwardness. Consider the characters when making the decision of finger puppet placement as well. For instance, the three bears most logically belong on one hand, while Goldilocks belongs on the other.

Finger puppets provide excellent fine motor exercise. To this end, young children may be introduced to finger puppets using only one per hand, adding puppets as the children develop fine motor skills.

FIG 2-1 Mouse, Rabbit, and Mole finger puppets (Sandy Mason's hand)

Hand Puppets

The most common hand puppet is the glove puppet. The body of the puppet resembles a glove or mitten. The puppet is operated by positioning the hand so that one or more middle fingers operate the head, with the remaining fingers operating the arms. [FIGURE 2-2] Many adults find this style of puppet awkward to manipulate. It is easy to see why children may find it particularly difficult.

The easiest type of hand puppet to operate is commonly called a mouth puppet because the mouth opens and shuts by separating the thumb and fingers. [FIGURE 2-3] This puppet is easier to operate and many teachers find it especially appropriate for the classroom. Mouth puppets assist in developing fine motor skills by encouraging children to keep their four fingers together while bending the wrist and moving the thumb. When children speak and move their hands using a hand puppet with a mouth, they are practicing hand-eye, hand-mouth coordination.

FIG 2-2 Clown glove puppet (traditional hand puppet with hand position)

FIG 2-3 Isadora Duck (mouth puppet with hand position)

Ingrid: In a kindergarten class I once observed, a teacher named Mrs. Brown put on a store-bought dog puppet. The puppet was made of rubber and the mouth stayed open unless the puppeteer squeezed hard to close it. Mrs. Brown addressed the class with the dog saying, "Good morning, boys and girls. How are you?" Although the teacher spoke clearly, the puppet's mouth never really closed. A little boy named Johnny stood up and said with great frustration, "Mrs. Brown, I can't understand the puppet."

(continued on page 14)

FIG 2-4 Ingrid with Romano the Lion (mouth and glove puppet)

Thanks to the wonderful Muppets, two other styles of hand puppets are well known. The hand and glove puppet is operated by one [FIGURE 2-4] or two puppeteers, as is the hand and rod puppet. [FIGURE 2-5]

Perhaps the easiest but most frequently overlooked hand puppet is just that: the puppeteer's hand. An example of this technique, appropriate for early childhood fine-motor skills, is described in chapter 6 of this book under "The Anything Puppet" on page 128 and "Jack and the Beanstalk" on page 106.

(continued from page 13) *Operating a puppet is creating the illusion that an inanimate object can see, hear, talk, walk, and breathe. Poor Mrs. Brown had a poorly made puppet. That dog didn't look a bit like it could talk. (Just try talking with your mouth open wide.) The unintelligible sounds produced by trying to talk without closing your mouth are what little Johnny heard from the dog, even though Mrs. Brown had spoken clearly. His teacher had not created the illusion of talking, so his eyes had "tricked" his ears into not understanding the words.*

FIG 2-5 Ingrid with Puppet-Ingrid (hand and rod puppet), created by Barry Gordemer

Rod Puppets

Rod puppets are pushed and pulled by rods, usually from below the puppet. This is probably the oldest style of puppet, and examples of rod puppets can be found in cultures around the world. Also called stick puppets, this is the easiest puppet for young children to operate, because it is so simple. [FIGURE 2-6] When a second rod controls the puppet's hand, the child puppeteer must move his two hands independently. This movement, which requires crossing the body midline, assists in developing motor skills. It also encourages a twisting movement with the wrist, like turning a knob on and off. An example of this is demonstrated when the puppet turns around or says no with its whole body. Butterfly, bat, or bird puppets encourage children to move their wrists up and down to flap wings. This wrist action is a helpful emergent literacy exercise as it works hand and wrist muscles needed for writing. [FIGURE 2-7]

FIG 2-6 Mr. Tiger (simple rod puppet for two hands)

FIG 2-7 Bat (simple, one-handed rod puppet)

Shadow Puppets

Shadow puppets are basically flat rod puppets. The puppet is held against a screen made of stretched fabric. A lamp casts light on the flat puppet so its shadow can be seen on the other side of the screen. [FIGURE 2-8] Fine motor skills are supported when students hold the puppet in one hand and move a part of the puppet with the other hand.

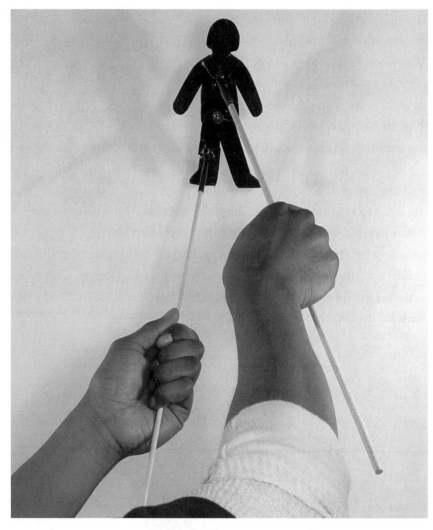

FIG 2-8 Little Girl shadow puppet (held by Aaron Mason)

Ingrid: This text does not address shadow puppets, but I love using them in the classroom. A book that I frequently reference on the subject is Worlds of Shadow *by David and Donna Wisniewski.*

Marionettes or String Puppets

Marionettes are operated from above by pulling on strings attached to the puppet. These puppets can have as few as two or four strings [FIGURE 2-9] or many more. Marionettes are most successfully operated by adults and older children, as the coordination required to manipulate the strings is often beyond the capabilities of those in early childhood. Small children love to watch marionettes, but because the hands are so far removed from the puppet they may be inclined to believe that the figure has magically come to life.

FIG 2-9 Elephant marionette (held by Ron Mason)

Object Puppets

The manipulation of an item not originally meant to be a puppet creates an object puppet. For example, a teacher may pull food out of a grocery bag to tell a story that focuses on the subject of nutrition. The apple may sing and dance in the teacher's hands, and the candy bar may "speak" in an arrogant and self-important way. Objects may be more effective as puppets when stick-on eyes are applied. [FIGURE 2-10] Object puppets often rely on symbolism and consequently support emergent literacy skills. A box becomes a prince or a carrot becomes a rocket ship. In this way, object puppets are particularly age appropriate as young children learn that one thing can stand for another.

FIG 2-10 Farm Girl (watering can puppet)

Ingrid: I think I did the best puppet show of my life once when I was stranded in Grand Central Terminal. I was there with a crowd of people, including families with children waiting for a train. I began an impromptu puppet story using the things I was traveling with. A sewing machine became a castle, a gargoyle figure became the superhero, and I made a dragon from upholstery fabric. I ended up using a lot of things from my purse too— the princess was a pair of scissors. I started out doing this for a handful of children, but when I was done, hundreds of people clapped!

Hat Puppets

While hat puppets are not traditionally considered one of the basic six types of puppets, they are more frequently and successfully used in the early childhood classroom and therefore have earned a place in a discussion of puppets used with young children. Hat puppets are usually designed to sit on top of the head and do not obscure the face. Their design denotes a particular character. For instance, a leopard hat puppet may feature spots, ears, and a nose with whiskers that sits on the puppeteer's forehead. Frequently, hat puppets do not include mouths, as there is often no space for them and no need for them. Hat puppets are often compared to masks, but there are two differences. The obvious distinction is that masks cover the face and hat puppets do not. This makes the puppets more appropriate for use with young children as they are less likely to be frightened. Second, masks are used by actors; the entire body portrays the character represented by the mask. However, hat puppets are operated by puppeteers by bobbing, tilting, and turning the head. The character remains in the puppet rather than being taken on by the puppeteer's whole body. Hat puppets are also the only puppets that consistently encourage use of motor skills in the neck and head. [FIGURE 2-11]

FIG 2-11 Aaron Mason models the Dog hat puppet

Ways Teachers Use Puppets

Classroom puppet uses are divided into two categories: puppets primarily manipulated by the teacher and puppets used by the children. When the goal is classroom control or more teacher-centered activities such as introducing a topic, then a puppet manipulated by the teacher is the best choice. Several options are described below.

Teacher Assistant

The teacher assistant is a recurring character in the classroom that acts much like a sidekick in a movie or television show. The puppet becomes so familiar to the students that they interact with it much as they would with the teacher. This situation has two advantages. First, you can be in two places at one time. You can be in the manipulatives corner working with a small group, while one or two other students can be reading a book to the puppet in the book corner. Second, the puppet can do the "dirty work" of teaching. For instance, the puppet can talk to you and say, "You know what? This class is really noisy. Do you think we'll get in trouble if we go into the hallway and make this much noise?" Most children will quiet down to hear the conversation and the situation will not require intervention on your part, making the puppet particularly effective as the disciplinarian. Because this puppet takes on a continuous, adult role in the classroom, it is important that it is operated only by the adults and never by the students.

Task Assistant

Task assistant puppets are similar to teacher assistants in that they aid in classroom management. However, these puppets are designed to help with a particular task or transition, such as lining up, cleanup, or preparing for naptime. Teachers may select puppets that reflect the task to be addressed. For example, gluing eyes on a dust mop or converting a cleaning implement with a handle into a rod puppet motivates students to clean up. Being asked by a broom to clean up is much more fun that being asked to do so by a teacher. [FIGURE 2-12]

Ingrid: Ms. Joanie had a class of kindergartners who were very loud. Joanie didn't want to suppress the enthusiasm, just the decibels. She bought a puppet and replaced the ears with enormous ears that she made. Then she introduced the character and explained how Sam could hear better than most people, but that loud noises really hurt his ears. The rest of circle time that day was spent doing listening exercises. Finally, Joanie put Sam on a stand on her desk, and told the children that Sam would live there all year. Later, when the class got loud, Joanie put earmuffs on Sam's ears so the noise wouldn't hurt him. The noise level gradually decreased without Joanie saying a word. Eventually, the children began talking to Sam even while he was sitting on his stand. He developed a personality, and became a part of the classroom community.

Ingrid: Thirty years ago before most children had preschool experience, I was working with a kindergarten teacher who had twenty-eight students, and no aide. Order and organization were real difficulties for this teacher. Even lining up was a problem for the class. To address this issue, I made a hand and rod puppet named Officer Alice. Alice had one arm that was a cardboard tube with a carpenter's spring-loaded measuring tape running through it. The puppet's hand was sewn to the end of the tape measure. When the measuring tape hand was pulled, the tape extended. After demonstrating how the arm worked, the police officer taught the children how to line up along her arm. It was the line leader's job to extend the arm and check the line to make sure it was straight. With Officer Alice, children couldn't wait to line up every day. Eventually, the teacher and I put numbers on the arm at the right intervals for the line, and the line leader would call the children to stand next to their number for the day. This became a wonderful way to learn number identification while lining up.

Ingrid: I told the story of Officer Alice at a workshop and two teachers thought of using a measuring tape as a snail. It would work just like Officer Alice's arm, and the snail could be used in a unit on gardening.

Specialty Puppet

A specialty puppet is one that is bought or made to help illustrate a specific unit. Examples would include a cow puppet that introduces a unit on farm animals, a dinosaur for a dinosaur unit, a puppet of the letter *B* to teach that letter and phoneme, or a chef puppet to discuss nutrition.

FIG 2-12 Michele Valeri holds Shelly Duster (a task puppet)

Puppet as Student

Children love to correct their elders. Using a puppet allows the children to reinforce what they know by correcting a character without diminishing your status as the authority figure. For example, an alien puppet that just came to this planet knows nothing of the preschool classroom. The children must teach it the appropriate way to wash hands, hold a hand up to speak, and listen quietly to instructions. In teaching the puppet, the children reinforce the material for themselves. Puppets used as students also are useful for reviewing lessons. A teacher might say, "Polly Puppet wasn't here yesterday when we were talking about vegetables. Who can show Polly which plants in this picture are vegetables?" In addition to aliens and puppets that missed lessons, puppets used as students can be forgetful and silly characters or babies that need to learn everything from scratch.

The puppet as student is an excellent way to employ the "cloze" technique as well. Teachers use the cloze technique when they begin a well-known story or phrase, or begin to impart a piece of information that the children know. At a crucial point in the sentence, the teacher stops, creating a pregnant pause that the children can fill by calling out the appropriate anticipated phrase. For example, a forgetful clown might say, "Yup, yup, and then Goldilocks tried the wee, tiny, teeny, little, bitty baby bear's porridge. And she said, 'This porridge is not too hot. This porridge is not too cold. It is . . .'" and generally the children will volunteer, "Just right!" The cloze technique is used to assess the children's knowledge of facts or stories, to encourage anticipated language, and to involve the children in the storytelling process. An example of the cloze technique used by a puppet would be when the character says, "I know, after lunch we're supposed to . . . um . . ." leaving an opportunity for the children to fill in the blank.

Reward Puppet

A puppet is a wonderful way to reward students for good behavior or completed tasks. When the class does something you want to encourage, bring out a favorite puppet that only appears on these special occasions: "When we finish cleaning up, we can all talk to Buddy Bear."

Ways Children Use Puppets

If you want to promote more child-centered activities that assist in developing creative thought, fine motor skills, or language, you might decide to provide puppets for the children to use. In this case, you will still operate a puppet for modeling purposes, but the emphasis is on helping the children express themselves through the puppets.

Student Task Puppets

Just as teachers may employ puppets to help with teaching tasks, certain puppets may be assigned to student tasks as well. For example, once you model the use of the meteorologist puppet, the "helper of the day" can use it with the class weather chart during morning circle time.

Puppet Actors

You might collect puppets that allow the children to act out a particular story they have in mind. Or, you might introduce two or three puppets, outline a problem that these puppets have, and then discuss with the children how it could be solved. The class then acts out the resulting story. In either case, you should discuss with the children what will happen and what the puppets will say, and model how the puppet is to be handled and how that character behaves. It is possible to provide a developmentally appropriate activity in which children present a story told with puppets. This kind of storytelling is facilitated by you and does not have an audience. Children should never be handed a puppet and be asked to make a presentation with no discussion or directions beforehand. This can result in a meandering story with no discernible plot, if a story results at all. If your goal is to provide a creative play experience with puppets, then place puppets in a classroom center as described below.

Unstructured Play

Puppets can be placed in the housekeeping area, the block area, or any other appropriate center in the classroom to encourage creative play. In order for them to be constructive instruments for learning, how-

Ingrid: I have noticed and discussed the "white hair phenomenon" with many people who have white hair themselves. Very young children are attracted to white hair out of curiosity and a natural appreciation for grandma and grandpa types. Young, fascinated children often came up to my white-haired mother. Many other people with white hair have told me they have had the same experience. I wanted to work with this phenomenon, so I created several older characters. One way I use them is to address "legalism," the phase in which children insist that there is a definite right and wrong in all things, and therefore there is only one way to tell a familiar story. These grandmother characters knew so much about the story. I might have Grandmother say: "Did you know that Goldilocks had a cousin named Juanita who had an adventure with four bears? There was a papa bear, a mama bear, a baby bear, and their Uncle Louie who was visiting just about the time Juanita got lost in the woods."

ever, there must be some discussion of their use. One option is to put out puppets already used in a puppet show for further exploration and storytelling. Because their use has been modeled, the children will have further ideas about what might be appropriately done with them. If puppets that have not been used in a show are left in a center for free choice time, they must be discussed with the children first. Proper handling and suggestions for use must be demonstrated. You need not assign the puppet a personality or provide details about it. These things can be done by the children's imaginations once they know how to operate the puppet.

Puppet Characters

In addition to selecting the puppet's purpose in the classroom, you must assign it an appropriate character. There are four major character categories: people, animals, fantasy characters such as monsters and aliens, and inanimate objects. Once you decide on the purpose of the puppet as described above, you will select a character type to carry out the goal. For instance, if your goal is bus safety, you might select or make a specialty puppet named Gladys the Bus Driver. In many cases it is not imperative that you select a specific character. A teaching assistant puppet can be any character type; however, in some situations the choice of character type will have a direct impact on the success in attaining the goal. For this reason, it is important to consider the options available when selecting character type.

People Characters

People puppets are popular and can be obtained in a variety of shapes, sizes, colors, and ages. As discussed above, a baby or toddler puppet makes an excellent character in the category of puppet as student. Child puppets are useful in addressing social and emotional issues because children identify with them. Parent puppets often represent authority figures. Older puppets are especially popular among young children as sympathetic characters.

Animal Characters

Animal puppets are probably used most frequently in classrooms. Animals are well loved by children and fit many units of study and curriculum goals. They can be used as specialty puppets (dogs for a unit on pets, cows for a unit on dairy products, or squirrels for a unit on backyard animals), task puppets (a raccoon to help children remember how to wash their hands, or a pack rat to help the children sort and classify classroom materials), or reward puppets (a big wet, slurpy lick from a dog for a job well done). In fact, animal characters can be used in any of the ways listed above. They can be especially useful in a multiethnic, multiracial classroom, as they look no more or less like any of the students, allowing each child to identify with the character at the same level.

If you select an animal puppet, think carefully about whether the animal will be presented realistically (a cat on all fours that meows) or anthropomorphized (a cat that walks on two legs and speaks and behaves like a person). Either portrayal is acceptable, but in the latter

Ingrid: I also have a Gramma Lion who tells stories and wears a shawl, bonnet, and wire-rim glasses. I use her as a task puppet to review stories the children already know. When Gramma Lion tells a story, she usually gets the facts confused. This gives the class an opportunity to correct her, and review the events and sequence of the story.

FIG 2-13 Ingrid with Gramma Romano (hand and rod puppet)

case young children who may not have experienced that animal before will be confused about how the animal truly behaves. This can further blur the line between fantasy and reality that eludes most young children. If that is a concern, the puppeteer may want to bring in a real animal to show the class before introducing the puppet versions. This is often impractical, so plastic animals, videotapes, and nonfiction books can give the students an idea of what the animal is really like. Then you can discuss imagination and pretend, explaining that the fish puppet is not like a real fish because the fish puppet can talk. (Taken from Cynthia Word's professional development workshop, "Dancing through the Day.")

Fantasy Characters

Fantasy characters such as monsters and aliens have been especially popular for the last thirty years thanks to Sesame Street. The Muppet monsters are nonthreatening and have proven effective in teaching concepts and skills. Fantasy characters are particularly useful in the category of puppet as student, and can be used in many other ways as well. However you use commercially purchased puppets of popular characters, be aware that the children may become fascinated by the puppet and unable to focus on the task at hand. Children become disenchanted if you can't re-create the voice, mannerisms, and personality of a beloved TV character. Even when you do a good impression of the character, the children will fixate on the fact that their favorite character has come to visit. Because the puppet is not in the familiar context, students will focus on the puppet itself, and not associate it with the chosen topic. Unless there is a specific reason to do otherwise, it is more successful for the teacher to choose an original puppet that is unfamiliar to the children. However, don't shy away from fantasy characters. They are excellent student puppets, and can be used as specialty puppets in addressing issues of fear and confusion.

Inanimate Object Characters

Inanimate objects are not limited to nonliving things, but for puppet purposes include plants as well, as we are unaccustomed to having them move, walk, and talk. You might use actual objects as puppets, alter or decorate actual objects to be puppets, or make object puppets from scratch. [FIGURE 2-14] Inanimate objects are best used as specialty puppets or as task puppets. With specialty puppets, for example, the puppet letter *B* teaches phonemes; the plant puppet teaches about locomotor versus nonlocomotor movement. Examples of task puppets might include a pointer with eyes that follows the words on the song charts, or a talking flame that teaches about fire safety. However, inanimate objects also can be used creatively in other categories; for instance, using a talking door to comment on the characters walking through it.

FIG 2-14 The Number 9 has moveable lips for speaking.

Ingrid: Pam was a first-grade teacher with a talking door she had made out of cardboard, with eyes that were hidden under smaller cardboard flaps on top. The mouth was an oven mitt that in its first life was shaped like a cow with a mouth. Pam had painted over the cow design, leaving the lips exposed. The door was a gatekeeper to the stories told in the classroom. The children asked questions to determine what story was going to be told:

Door: This wolf just walked through my door, and boy was he mad!
Child: Did a girl wearing a red hood go through you too?
Door: No.
Child: Can you ask the wolf if he has tried to eat pigs?

CHAPTER 3

Using Puppets in the Classroom

Qualities of the Classroom

ONCE YOU HAVE DEFINED the goal and selected the puppet character to address it, you should consider the qualities of the children in the class. There are three aspects of the child that are important when tailoring a lesson for a group:

1. The developmental level and capabilities of the class

2. The size of the group

3. The "chemistry" of the classroom and what classroom management style it needs

As with any other curricular tool, knowing your children well helps you make the best choices on their behalf.

Developmental Level of Class

Choosing developmentally appropriate material to use with puppets is no different from choosing other material for the classroom. You should take into account the curriculum being used, your knowledge of how children grow and mature, and the developmental level of the individuals in your group. In fact, using puppets can be a way to take otherwise inappropriate materials and make them developmentally suitable. For example, an overly long book can be edited by having the puppets act out the pertinent parts of the story.

Whether there are children who have been diagnosed with special needs in the classroom or not, you are encouraged to read chapter 5, "Puppets and Special Children," later in this book. Techniques used to make material appropriate for children with special needs work in a wide variety of settings, and most of you will find techniques to apply to your classes to create a successful puppet experience.

Class Size

You can add or subtract characters to suit the number of children in your class. One way to do this is to have multiple children play a given part. With the story of "The Three Little Pigs," for example, there can be three pigs in the house of straw, three in the house of sticks, two in the house of bricks, and four wolves pursuing them. Adding characters not seen in the book or story is another way to enlarge the cast. Three puppeteers can sell the straw, sticks, and bricks to the pigs. To decrease the number of parts, simply drop a character from the story; for example, do not mention the dog or the farmer's wife while presenting "The Farmer in the Dell." Another way to decrease the number of parts is to simply give students two puppets each.

Alternatively, performing the play twice provides the students with an opportunity to experience both being a puppeteer and being an audience member. If you decide to use this approach, begin by explaining that everyone will get a chance to be in the audience and to be a puppeteer as well. Spend a few minutes discussing the job of each group, encouraging the students to realize that the audience should pay attention, listen respectfully, and clap at the end if they enjoyed the presentation. Performers must wait for their turn to receive and operate the puppet, hold up their puppet, and speak loudly enough for the audience to hear. It must be emphasized that if a performance atmosphere is chosen, it should remain age appropriate in its execution. Children should not be asked to memorize lines, there should be no pressure to participate, and everyone should be involved at all times, either as an audience member or a puppeteer.

Classroom Management

Throughout this book the reader will find a number of puppet techniques that may assist the teacher in classroom management. Because they are described in detail in other parts of this book, they will not be detailed here. However, some are listed below as a reminder of how puppets can be used to address management issues through a variety of techniques.

- Using a silent puppet to encourage turn-taking and listening skills (page 45)

- Using puppets as transition tools between the activities

- Using a puppet to reward children for positive behavior (page 22)

- Using a puppet to give children corrective directions (page 20)

- Altering puppet stimulus to suit the needs of the classroom (page 57)

- Using puppets to review class rules and appropriate behavior

- Using task puppets (page 20) and student task puppets to guide the children through a specific assignment

- Gradually introducing a puppet stimulus to maintain order in the classroom (page 57)

- Introducing a puppet to the child who will use it to encourage creativity and discourage inappropriate use (page 36)

- Using a defined space for the puppet lesson (page 58)

These are only a few of the puppet techniques mentioned in this book to help teachers address the particular personality of a classroom. There are many more, and teachers may use puppets to create their own methods to use with children.

Meeting the needs of a particular group of students is not limited just to classroom management. A teacher may conclude that the children in his room need to think more creatively and work on their problem-solving skills. Another teacher may decide that his class has not been exposed to the life experiences that most five-year-olds have. Yet another teacher may decide that his group needs to learn to work more independently. All of these and many more classroom needs can be addressed through puppets.

Puppet Rules for the Classroom

Selecting Puppets Carefully

Before choosing a puppet character, ask yourself, "What do I want to achieve by using a puppet? What kind of puppet will best assist me in reaching this goal?" Then choose a puppet personality that complements the goal for the classroom. Also be sure to pick out a puppet that is comfortable to operate. Review chapters 4 and 7 for ideas about selecting puppets.

Plan the Lesson

Start well ahead of the lesson by thinking about the content and what the puppet will say. Make notes on what the puppet will do during the lesson and run through the notes step by step to ensure that the lesson plan and the puppet's part in it are clear. One way to begin is to answer the following questions:

- Where will the puppet come from? Will it be pulled from the closet where it is stored, from a decorated box, or from a container indicative of the theme? For example, a flower puppet might come out of a flowerpot.

- How will you introduce the puppet? Will the students need to wake it up? Will it come out perky and loud to reflect the personality developed for it?

- What task will the puppet have? Will it introduce a topic, help review a lesson, or assist in an activity? Will it just tell an engaging story?

- How will the children respond? If the class is likely to be particularly hesitant in approaching the puppet, plan a strategy to pull them in. If you think a puppet might cause overexcitement and trigger unwanted behavior, build in some classroom management tools.

- Finally, how will the class time with the puppet come to an end? Will the puppet become sleepy and ask to take a nap? Will it go around and shake hands good-bye with each student?

Puppet lessons at circle time can be more easily planned if they are considered in four parts: beginning, middle, ending, and follow-up. However, when puppets are truly integrated into the classroom, this format may be used partially or not at all. If you have a task puppet that helps clean up the room during transitions, it isn't necessary after the first use of the puppet to include an introductory beginning, a closing activity, or a follow-up. Because puppets can be used in so many ways, the possible components of a lesson plan are listed here in the traditional categories. You might select one element from the format and use it alone or use several in a different order. When puppets are used to their fullest extent, these elements become "mix and match." Nor is this list complete. Most teachers find they are most successful when they add to, take away from, and alter the lesson plan to make it meaningful to their class.

The Beginning of the Lesson

Here are some ideas to spark your thinking on how to start the lesson:

- Introduce the topic to be addressed using props, concrete materials, and discussion.

- Introduce the puppet, its name, and its purpose in the lesson or the classroom.

- Introduce the rules of puppet use, including the puppet pledge (see Ingrid's story on page 36).

- Demonstrate the appropriate way to operate the puppet.

- Establish the atmosphere or setting. This includes giving the children the opportunity to use their imaginations to help enter the experience. You might ask them to "taste" invisible ice cream, "feel" the hot sun even while they are indoors, or "walk through the squishy sand." Before a lesson that is to take place under water, ask the children to splash imaginary water on their faces, let the waves lap against their legs, and smell the salt air. "Inviting the children into the pretending" gives them a chance to explore puppet uses in a limited way.

The Middle of the Lesson

The middle is the core of the lesson and might include versions of the following:

- Establish the problem to be solved, the character's dilemma, or the conflict of the story.

- Establish the sequence of events.

- Reaffirm the puppet's personality or attributes.

- Outline a problem to be solved.

- Act out an end to the story using the children's suggestions for resolution.

The End of the Lesson

Wrapping up the lesson can involve any of the following:

- Review the sequence or story.

- Tell the children what will happen next in a following session or at a later time.

- Praise the students for their participation.

- Create a ritual ending, like always waving good-bye to the puppet.

Follow-Up to the Lesson

After the lesson, consider following up in one of these ways:

- Put the puppets in a classroom center for use during free choice time.

- Read or tell the story again in another format (acting it out with the children, telling it using small illustrative props, and so on).

- Do other activities that support the curriculum goal addressed by the puppets.

- Repeat the activity.

When planning lessons, the ending of the lesson deserves special thought. Even a successful lesson can lose its efficacy with a weak or abrupt ending. Decide exactly how the lesson will end. At what point will the puppets and props be collected? Will it be done by the teacher or by students? Will the students bow? If so, they may need a demonstration of how to bow. Plan a ritual praise used in the classroom, such as, "Now give yourself a big pat on the back, and say, 'I did a good job today.'" Finally, you can interview the puppeteers. Hold a pen or other prop, pretending it's a microphone. Explain that you are pretending that people were watching the lesson, perhaps on TV, and they want to know more about it. You might say something like, "Welcome to Mr. Li's Famous Puppet Company! I know you all enjoyed the program today and want to meet a few of the famous puppeteers who participated in it. Shelley, can you tell our TV audience what it was like to be the 'bad guy' in this show? Emma, what was it like to wait for your turn to hold your puppet up? Jalen, what is the best part about being in a puppet show? James, what is your favorite part of the story you acted out?" It is rarely possible to have each child answer a question each time puppets are used. Just keep track of who had a chance to speak, allowing the interviewees to rotate among the class members over a number of lessons. This exercise strengthens oral communication skills, and gives students an opportunity to exercise higher-order thinking as they formulate and express their own opinions.

Show Children How to Use the Puppets

Before handing a puppet to any child, begin by introducing her to the puppet properly and by demonstrating appropriate handling.

If the children don't have a model on the appropriate operation of a puppet, it is more likely that they will use it as a weapon or try to take it apart. Begin by having a child hold out her hands and place the puppet on her palm. [FIGURE 3-1] Ask her to demonstrate a few simple movements, such as laughing, waving, or nodding. Then let her come up with her own movements and follow suggestions from classmates. Puppets can then be handed out to the whole class or to a small group of children for further demonstration. It is up to you to decide whether to mention the things that are not to be done with the puppet. While it is inadvisable to give the students ideas of inappropriate use that they would not have considered otherwise, some puppets lend themselves to inevitable misuse. Anticipate misuses, like hitting with the puppet, poking using a stick, or pulling off loose pieces on the puppet, and explain the consequences. This may save you both time and stress.

FIG 3-1 Christine Manor gives a simple rod puppet to Katharine T. Manor by putting the head stick in Katharine's right hand and the hand stick in Katharine's left hand.

Even if a puppet will be used only by an adult, that puppet should be carefully introduced. For example, you might say, "Class, my friend Sam the Dog came to visit us today." The puppet can wave, nod, or say hello. Then say, "Sam, would you like to say hello to the children?" and Sam might answer, "Yeah! I really like to be patted gently." Take the puppet around to each child to be touched or patted using two fingers. The puppet himself can remind a child who is too rough to try again.

Practice with Puppets

Before you use a particular puppet for the first time, practice in front of a mirror. Pretend that the mirror is the class and stand facing it. Remember to look at the puppet when it talks and react to what it is saying by nodding your head and commenting, "Uh-huh." Alternatively, ask another adult to watch the lesson before using it in the classroom. An objective adult or older child can give valuable feedback and provide you with the advantage of a "live audience."

Promote Children's Imagination

Never try to convince the children that a puppet is alive. Three- and four-year-olds have trouble discerning reality from fantasy and are animists who believe that anything moving must be alive. Do not confuse them just as they are beginning to understand this concept. Professional puppeteers may feel that some of the "magic" is lost when they admit that the puppet is not real. Teachers know that this is not the case at all. Because children are so willing to suspend disbelief, they can easily consider the puppet as an object being operated by their teacher, then happily react to it as if it were a real little boy or a dog. If a child says, "Hey, that's not a real dog!" respond by saying, "That's right. It's a puppet and we are pretending that it is real. I am going to move it and talk for it to help us pretend." To assist with this concept, talk about imagination with the children. Define it and give examples of how they use their imaginations in the classroom and on the playground.

Ingrid: I don't usually punish children for taking off an eye or some other piece of the puppet. I think a certain amount of curiosity is to be expected, and accidents will happen. Children are often embarrassed when a puppet breaks, and in that case I say, "Oops! That puppet needs to go to the puppet doctor." I always try to have extra puppets on hand for these situations. The exception to this is when a child is malicious and intentionally destructive. In this situation I would recommend using whatever disciplinary tools the teacher has already instituted in her classroom.

Maintain a Safe Atmosphere

As with any other classroom activity, work to maintain an atmosphere of safety and trust when you use puppets. The puppet must be introduced properly and a child should never be forced to touch the puppet. If a child does not want to speak to the puppet (which may be perceived as a stranger), ask if he would like to tell you first and then you will tell the puppet for him. Reward risk taking with a positive comment, but avoid drawing undue attention to children who may be uncomfortable with it. If a child gives a wrong answer, she can be offered a second chance, ask a friend for help, or be given a clue. No child should feel they have failed when playing with a puppet.

Ingrid: I've found it possible to bring in scary puppets or do scary things with a puppet as long as children first know they are in a supportive and safe atmosphere. Sometimes I take in a T-Rex baby puppet that some children find frightening because of the large pointy teeth. First I will lay the puppet on the floor and prove that it can't move unless I move it. Then we examine the puppet closely, counting its toes, letting the children touch the teeth to feel that they are soft, etc. Next I ask permission of the class to put the puppet on and make it talk. If a child says no, then I do not put it on. (It's only happened to me once in the seventeen years I've been doing it.) If no one objects, I put on the puppet and talk to him. The puppet answers in a gruff voice. If children get nervous, I take the puppet off and start over.

Eventually I let the children try to feed the T-Rex an imaginary hot dog. Sometimes, a child will go back to his seat and say, "That was really scary! You try it!" My friends call this "Ingrid's Preschool Roller Coaster Ride of Bravery."

The amount of preparation and planning necessary for puppet use is greater as you begin to develop lesson plans and experiment with puppets in the classroom. As with any teaching technique, less time is necessary for planning and preparation after you become more familiar with puppets and how they might be used. Regardless of the amount of time invested, the benefits of puppetry in the classroom are well worth the effort.

CHAPTER **4**

Puppet Faces and Stages

Developing a Puppet Personality Step by Step

OPERATING A PUPPET is creating the illusion that an inanimate object can see, hear, talk, walk, and breathe. This chapter addresses how to manipulate puppets to give the impression of life. While each aspect of manipulation is discussed in detail in this chapter, confidence as a puppeteer only comes with practice. The fortunate thing for teachers is that practice can become a part of the daily classroom routine.

FIG 4-1 There are a variety of styles of purchased and handmade eyes. (From left to right) Purchased animal eyes with no whites, purchased eyes with hand-cut whites added, handmade eyes, black beads for animal eyes, wiggle eyes with the pupils glued in place in the back before attaching, layered handmade eyes.

FIG 4-2 Baby eyes need to be close to the mouth and nose.

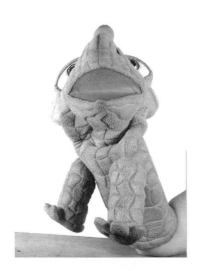

FIG 4-3 Sam needs to look at the audience (namely, the camera) to hold the interest of the children; not as shown in the photo. Here the puppeteer lifted her fingers to open the mouth, losing the focus of the eyes.

Eyes

With few exceptions, all puppets have eyes. The old cliché is true of both humans and puppets that "the eyes are the windows of the soul." They are the most important element of the puppet's face.

In human conversation the active participants look at one another: "Please look at me when I'm talking to you!" The same must be true when humans converse with puppets. When choosing a puppet, look at it carefully and check to see if the puppet is looking back. If a commercially made puppet is suitable but the eyes are not correct, felt eyes can be glued over the original eyes.

When making your own puppet or replacing the eyes on a commercially made puppet, always try to focus the eyes so that they look like they can see—that they aren't too far apart or too close together. Puppet eyes can be made from a variety of materials [FIGURE 4-1] and their placement can change the whole character or personality of the puppet. For example, putting the eyes far away from the nose and high on the forehead gives the impression of arrogance or intelligence. Putting the eyes close to the nose makes a puppet look like a baby or a young child. [FIGURE 4-2]

In addition to giving the puppet focus, you must be sure the puppet is looking at the audience. All puppeteers accidentally make their puppets look at the ceiling or the floor at one time or another. [FIGURE 4-3] It takes vigilance and practice to remember to point the eyes in the right direction. In a classroom situation when you are using a "sidekick" or teaching assistant, the puppet eyes need to look at the children. This requires you to move the puppet's head around to include all of the children in the classroom when it talks. If you are presenting a puppet play with a puppet in each hand, the puppet that is speaking should look at the audience, and the listening puppet should look at the speaking puppet.

Some people (especially actors who use a puppet) tend to act with their whole bodies, using overt facial expressions while only slightly moving the puppet. The puppeteer becomes more interesting than the puppet, and the illusion of animated life is lost. Puppeteers must focus their energy into the puppet to have a successful experience.

Mouths

Some puppets have moveable mouths and some do not. To make puppets without moveable mouths talk, wiggle and twist the puppet in a rhythm compatible with the speech. As long as the puppets move when they talk, are still when they don't talk, and maintain eye focus, there is really no wrong way to animate a puppet without a moveable mouth.

For more complex puppets with moveable mouths, puppet eye focus must be maintained. The easiest way to open a puppet's mouth is to raise the fingers. In doing so, the puppet's head moves up, and seems to be looking at the ceiling. In order to avoid the audience losing eye contact with the puppet, keep the fingers together and spread them away from the thumb vertically while dropping the thumb each time the puppet opens his mouth. The effect is that of the puppet "pushing" the words out of its mouth. [FIGURES 4-4, 4-5] Watching the puppetry performed with the Muppets is an excellent way to observe this technique.

As you practice speaking for your puppet there are two final things to incorporate. First, the volume of your voice should be reflected in the puppet's mouth movements. For example, open the puppet's mouth wide when it is shouting and only a little to indicate the puppet's whisper. Second, make sure the puppet closes its mouth between words.

While mastering lip sync is important for a puppeteer and perhaps useful for a teacher, the fact is that the least interesting thing mouth puppets can do is talk. There are a number of lively and entertaining activities you can add to your puppet repertoire. Some options are listed and described on the next page.

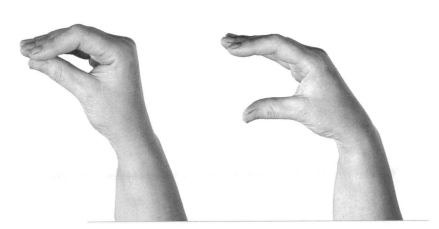

FIG 4-4 To make a hand puppet speak, start by holding the hand as shown here.
FIG 4-5 Then bend the wrist and drop the thumb.

Ingrid: I use a fainting puppet named Nervous Ned to address childhood fears and phobias. Ned faints when a spider surprises him. Because the element of surprise is scary to children, I have him react differently if he is told about the spider before he sees it. The children help Ned overcome his fears, even if they are scared. If appropriate to the class, I use a big, ugly rubber spider; otherwise, I use a friendly, silly puppet spider. I encourage the class to talk to Ned and they say things like, "Spiders won't hurt you, especially if you leave them alone."

Eating

Perhaps the most obvious alternative to speaking is eating. Eating takes place in three steps: the puppet first takes a bite, chews, and then swallows. Some puppets may be so ill mannered and noisy as to chomp and swallow at almost the same time! Puppets that eat can lead into lessons on nutrition and manners, as well as carnivorous and herbivorous animals. (When working with young children, the latter is especially popular when done with dinosaur puppets.) Children enjoy watching puppets eat in a loud and gregarious manner; conversely, a mouse or bird puppet might best demonstrate how to eat politely during snack.

Yawning

Yawning puppets can be helpful at naptime. Some characters may yawn with a huge, gaping mouth that stretches open for a long time. Others may have small, delicate yawns. Yawning is the one case in which it is appropriate for the puppet to lose eye focus with its audience. Just as people throw their heads back and lose eye contact when they yawn, puppets may do the same. Puppet yawns are as contagious as people yawns, and help get children in the mood for rest time.

Snoring

While a snoring puppet amuses children, it is not something that should be demonstrated before naptime. Most children find the sound and action of snoring funny and exciting, and therefore snoring is best saved for center or circle time.

Sneezing

A sneezing puppet can be an excellent way to teach students to use tissues and dispose of them properly. A conversation between the teacher and a puppet might go as follows:

Puppet: Oh no! I have to sneeze!

Teacher: Oh dear. Everyone cover your ears. My puppet Herman sneezes very loudly.

Puppet: Ah, ah, ah, ah, chooooooooo!

Teacher:	Herman, you sneezed all over everyone!
Puppet:	Yeah, I know.
Teacher:	That's not nice. You spread germs that way.
Puppet:	Yeah, I know.
Teacher:	What do you have to say for yourself?
Puppet:	*(Blows his nose on the teacher's sleeve, making a loud raspberry noise.)*
Teacher:	Herman, that is disgusting. Who can show Herman how he should cover his nose when he sneezes? Can you do it yourself? Who can show Herman how he should blow his nose?

The louder and more disgusting the puppet is, the more the children enjoy it. This lesson in hygiene can be reviewed by using other puppets that cough or sneeze, and the students can correct them.

Hiccuping

Young children also find hiccups funny. The puppeteer may even choose to have the puppet say the word *hiccup* while they are hiccuping.

Fainting

Puppets all over the world faint with their mouths open. While some puppets open their mouths with a gasp and fall quickly, others are slow and graceful when they fall.

Laughing

The last and perhaps best thing to do with a puppet's mouth is laugh. Laughing in a realistic, believable fashion may be difficult for actors. However, puppets don't laugh like people—they laugh like puppets! An excellent example of puppet laughter is Ernie from Sesame Street. When watching Ernie laugh, notice how the head and body bob up and down in rhythm with the laughing sound. This movement is the universal puppet laughing movement. Although it is universal, laughing sounds can be very different. For example, some puppets laugh through their teeth and make a hissing sound. Others laugh with their lips closed, making a humming sound. A favorite laugh is the "shotgun

Ingrid: I was in a kindergarten classroom near the end of the year, and the kids were obsessed with telling jokes. The teacher was well aware that the jokes weren't really funny, but she was thrilled that all the children—even the shy ones—wanted to practice their language skills, even if the jokes were silly. At the beginning of each class, four children were chosen to tell jokes to my Gramma Lion puppet. Of course, she thought they were the funniest things she'd ever heard, and her laughter rewarded the children for taking verbal risks.

Ingrid: I tried an experiment using my normal speaking voice in three consecutive classes one day. In the first class, I used a mother giraffe puppet with my voice, and the children accepted the characterization. In the second class, the children also accepted my normal speaking voice. In the third class, one little boy said, "Puppet Lady, that puppet talks like you!" I said, "Yes, the giraffe talks just like me, because I'm making the puppet talk. Now we're going to do a puppet show, and this time the puppet will sound just like you, because you are going to make it talk." As a result, each child was enthusiastic about using their own voice with the puppet.

laugh." This laugh begins when the puppet silently bobs up and down with the usual laughing movement while his mouth is closed tightly. The puppeteer says something like, "Oh, no! My puppet has a laugh stuck inside him." Finally the puppet opens his mouth with one loud "HA!" Teachers using puppets in the classroom will want to choose a laugh sound to fit the puppet's personality. Giants or very large puppets may laugh with their mouths wide open with the sound "HO, HO, HO!" Little characters might laugh while covering their tiny mouths and making a "Tee-hee-hee" sound with high-pitched voices. The teacher's ability to make the puppet laugh adds to her ability to relate to the class with the puppet. When a child says something clever and the classroom puppet laughs, he is rewarded for his language skills and feels gratified in taking the verbal risk.

Voices

Everyone can speak in the upper register of their voice, in the lower register of their voice, and in their normal register. These three pitches alone can fit a number of puppet characters. High-pitched voices are good for small animal characters, children, and babies. Deep voices are good for large animals, giants, and authority figures. When a teacher uses her own voice, children usually do not notice that the puppet and the teacher sound the same. If a child does point it out, the teacher can say, "That's right, because I'm making the puppet talk. I'm glad you noticed."

In addition to these three pitches, there are several simple techniques that give the puppeteer more character voices. The first is to alter the speed at which the puppet is talking. For example, a turtle puppet may speak very slowly. This can be especially effective in eliciting anticipated speech from the children using the cloze technique. In order to do this, a puppeteer would have her puppet say very slowly, "Hello, boys and . . ." The children will fill in, saying "girls" well before the turtle very slowly intones "girls." In addition to supporting language learning, children find this particularly funny. You can take the exercise even further by having the turtle say, "I am very . . ." and the children will offer responses, such as "slow," "hungry," or "sleepy." This either becomes a jumping-off point for the children to create their own story or scenario with the turtle, or the turtle can offer his own slow answer, "green." After the children's answers, his deadpan answer again seems very funny to the children. Children also find fast talk amusing, but to be successful at it, the puppeteer must practice.

If you speak a language other than English or can use an authentic accent, this can enrich your collection of puppet characters. Children love to hear another language being spoken; however, it is important to avoid stereotypes when using accents. This can easily be done by using an accent that you are familiar with in your own heritage.

Another opportunity to develop voices for your puppets comes from listening and imitating voices heard in cartoons, movies, and other medias. This provides ideas for creating identifiable voice characteristics. For example, John Wayne's speech patterns are readily identifiable, and relatively easy to replicate. Two other vocal changes that most people can make are "denasal" (talking as if your nose is stopped up) and stretching out short words, as in, "Ohhh, I don't know what to sayyyyyeeee."

As you build a collection of voices to use with puppets, do not overlook the puppet whisper. The whisper can be a powerful tool for classroom management. In order to hear the puppet, the children must quiet down.

Perhaps the most effective puppet for creativity and classroom management is the silent puppet. This is a puppet that only whispers in the teacher's ear, or has a small voice that must be held next to the listener's ear to be heard. Tell the children that the puppet is too shy to speak out loud and that the puppet will whisper what he wants to say only to you. Then report what the puppet is saying to the group. Children can anticipate what the puppet is going to say and are attentive in order to find out what the shy, quiet puppet has to communicate.

While in some cases you may use a quiet or silent puppet, in other situations you may increase the volume and use a loud voice. This change in volume may be for characters such as giants, lions, or bears.

Not all characters speak with words. For instance, a duck puppet may only quack and you must interpret: "Fortunately, I speak fluent duck!" A conversation might go like this:

Teacher: Good morning class. I have a friend who wants to meet you today. This is Isadora Duck.

Duck: Quack, quack, quack, quack, quack, quack.

Teacher: She said, "Good morning, boys and girls."

Ingrid: I have a dinosaur puppet named Gabby the Gallimimus. The Gallimimus is thought to be among the fastest of all dinosaurs. I like to reflect that fact in her speech, making her talk very fast and then every once in a while draw one word out slowly.

Ingrid: My friend Mike told me that after reading a book at circle time, a very shy child whom he had never heard speak said that she had something to tell Sam, his silent puppet. Mike took Sam out, and the little girl told Sam the whole story she had heard at circle time, saying, "I liked when the brown dog splashed and when he ate hot dogs and when he scratched."

Ingrid: My friend and colleague Michele Valeri uses a special task puppet, Julius, to help with classroom management and listening skills. Julius is shy and prefers to listen rather than speak. Julius becomes a model for listening, and allows students to anticipate language while they wait for his "whispers" in Michele's ear to be recounted out loud for them. Julius describes this technique later in chapter 6.

Duck:	**Quack, quack.**
Teacher:	**Isadora just said, "I'm sad."**
Duck:	**Quack, quack, quack, quack, quack.**
Teacher:	**She can't go swimming!**

You must quack with the same inflections and emotion that would be used in translated speech using one quack per syllable. A two-syllable word like *morning* would be two short quacks, while the word *good* would be one longer quack. After becoming used to the quacks, children begin to "understand" what the duck is saying as long as it uses simple, logical sentences and the children can understand the feelings conveyed through the quacks—sad quacking, angry quacking, and so on. This technique is not limited to ducks. A cow might moo during a unit on nutrition and dairy products, or a dog might bark his way through a classroom conversation about pets.

If you use this technique, be prepared for the child who hears the animal say something totally unexpected. Sometimes this can be a wonderful contribution, such as when a child says something that takes the class on an improvised adventure. Occasionally, the child will say something revealing, such as, "The duck says she is mad that she didn't get to go to the paint center." Such comments may be worth investigating to help address the child's own situation or feelings. Also, if you are trying to introduce a specific topic or concept, a student's unexpected translation might take you off in a direction you are unwilling or unable to go. In this case, you must be prepared to table those comments for later discussion, or perhaps use a different puppet technique that does not allow for as much uncontrolled creativity on the children's part.

Another choice is to use puppets with no voice at all. Nonverbal puppets differ from silent puppets in that they do not whisper to the puppeteer or talk so the children can't hear. Instead, they communicate solely through body movement, costumes, and props. Nonverbal puppets work well with children who have hearing impairments or a speech delay, as well as being an excellent introduction to puppetry in general.

FIG 4-6 Julius whispers to Michele Valeri

Selecting an appropriate voice is important for two reasons. First, the more interesting and compelling the voice, the more the children will be engaged with the puppet; the more they are engaged with the lesson, the more likely they will learn from the experience. While you may not achieve all of the learning goals with a particular puppet lesson—even when all of the children are engaged and participating—the odds are much greater than if the children are not engaged at all. Puppet voices can aid in this goal.

Second, young children are learning to identify, name, process, and respond to varied emotions both in themselves and in others. Working with puppet voices allows children to isolate the emotional cues communicated aurally. Because simple puppets can only portray two or three emotions visually, the child must rely on the tone, speed, and volume of the puppeteer's voice to interpret emotion. This skill can be translated into their daily lives. A lesson that includes puppets saying the same words with different inflections to convey emotion emphasizes this benefit.

Bodies

The wonderful thing about puppets is that they only need as many body parts as are required for an activity. A puppet might only need a head or a head and arms. In some cases, only one arm needs to be animated. The other might be stuffed and hanging or attached to the body or prop. Puppet legs are sometimes animated, sometimes not. Some arms and legs are attached so that they move or jiggle easily when manipulated by the puppeteer. These wiggly, jiggly arms and legs can be created with Slinkies. This is especially effective for young children, as they are able to create the impression of life with fine motor skills typical of their age. [FIGURE 4-7]

Unlike eyes or mouths, puppet bodies do not need to be created or animated specifically in order to create the impression of life. When working with rod puppets, children may just move the body as they speak and hold the puppet still when not speaking to successfully indicate animation. No moving parts are necessary; in fact, no body is necessary if it is not needed.

Ingrid: My grandmother lived in the Badlands of Montana. People in that part of Montana speak loudly in general, but my grandmother's next-door neighbor was the loudest woman I'd ever known. I was scared stiff of her, until I was a teenager and discovered that she was one of the sweetest people who ever lived.

I think many shy children are afraid of adults who speak loudly. Now I use loud puppets with humor to help children overcome their fear of loud talkers. One example is in "Jamal and Mr. Bear" (see the lesson plan found in chapter 6, page 72), where I always make Mr. Bear's voice loud, and then Jamal discovers what a kind animal the bear is.

FIG 4-7 The Slinky Spider

Whether you choose a whispering ant, shouting giant, or quacking duck, it is important to be comfortable with what you have chosen. Comfort and confidence set the stage for the most important elements of all for a puppeteer: playfulness and fun.

Puppet Stages

The trend in modern American professional puppetry is to eliminate or minimize traditional puppet staging. Like the Japanese Bunraku tradition of never hiding the puppeteer, American puppeteers are increasingly performing in full view of the audience (here termed "exposed puppetry"). On TV, for example, the puppeteer is still hidden. Special effects, camera work, and video "tricks" have made it difficult for some puppeteers working on the small screen to compete, feeling that the

FIG 4-8 Children from the Stoddert Cooperative Play Program watch Michele and Danny the baby Diplodocus.

traditional puppet stage is too restrictive in comparison. In theatrical settings, however, elaborate marionette stages are being replaced with a puppeteer standing in full view while the marionette performs on a simple platform. Hand puppets appear on the puppeteer's hand and the audience watches as the puppeteer's lips move. In the classroom there are few disadvantages to this more revealing form of puppet presentation. The puppeteer rarely distracts the audience, even though she is not hiding behind a stage. [FIGURES 4-8, 4-9] In fact, there are some definite advantages to exposed puppets. Children who witness puppetry without stages may play more freely with their own puppets in any given space. The time and expense of setting up a puppet stage is unnecessary; however, try not to be limited to only one space in the room.

Although the emphasis is on using puppets imaginatively in the classroom, children enjoy puppet stages, much as they like playing with a dollhouse or a fort. Occasionally, children ignore puppet stages set up in the classroom. If this is the case, a reexamination of puppet introductions or puppets themselves may encourage use of the stage. Further, you should examine the stage to evaluate its usefulness in the classroom. Is the stage large enough to hold more than two children? Is the opening small and therefore limiting? Is the stage too tall or too short for the children?

In addition to the traditional stage (or as a substitution for it), non-traditional stages and exposed puppetry can expand the possibilities

FIG 4-9 Children from the Stoddert Cooperative Play Program watch Michele and Danny the baby Diplodocus.

Ingrid: My five-year-old friend Jake performs puppet shows all the time, and his activities reflect his exposure to a wide variety of live and TV puppet performances. In presenting "The Three Billy Goats Gruff," the couch became the stage; a Lego table and a footstool were the supports for a bridge made from the lid of a plastic storage box. The troll was a tube of paper with a wad of crumbled paper taped loosely to it. The smallest goat was a bent toy called a Toober, and the middle-sized goat was a plush American buffalo toy. Jake himself was the big goat, using a reindeer headband with antlers left over from Christmas. The back of the couch was the hill the goats went over. The troll lived under the storage box lid, and when Jake (as the biggest goat) ran into the troll, the crumpled paper troll's head fell off to create a special effect. This is children's puppet play at its best, demonstrating Jake's problem-solving skills using the materials on hand.

for teaching and learning. The traditional appliance box with a hole can be restrictive and frustrating. To address these concerns, stages should be considered creatively as children themselves are creative in their use of them.

In the classroom, a variety of flat surfaces can be puppet stages, including bookshelves, kitchen furniture, or tabletops. No matter what the stage is, you should show the children how to use it as a stage. As a result, children can "play puppet show" and the possibilities are endless.

Stages can also be fashioned from cheap cardboard, sawhorses, or wood. In creating your own stage, there are five principles for sizing:

1. The stage should be the approximate waist height of the average child in the classroom.

2. There should be room for four to five children behind the stage.

3. At least one side of the stage should be lower or higher to give the children options.

4. The stage must be stable and safe so it will not fall over.

5. There should be a shelf (called a puppet play board) at least 10 inches wide for props and other objects. Puppets perform behind this shelf, and can then put the props down as part of the performance.

Another possibility for a stage is clear plastic stretched between two poles. The advantage to this type of stage is that puppets behind it are distorted for the audience, similar to objects seen through water. [FIGURE 4-10] This works well for presentations of stories like *The Rainbow Fish, In a Small Small Pond, A House for Hermit Crab,* or *Big Al.* While the puppeteer is visible, he is not a distraction behind the clear curtain, and the vinyl can be painted with acrylic seaweed and rocks to create an underwater scene. To make an underwater stage, use a clear shower curtain or a piece of vinyl sheeting purchased from a fabric store or a department store. The poles can be old broomsticks or 1-inch PVC plumbing tubing bought at a hardware store. The vinyl or plastic can be glued, taped, fastened with Velcro, or stapled to the poles. In the latter case, the edges of the plastic must first be reinforced with duct tape, and then stapled.

Even more important than the stage used is the story atmosphere. This can be done with any of the stages above, or it can be done with props, sound effects, or other sensory stimuli. For example, a puppet presentation of *The Rainbow Fish* could be done using the shower curtain stage described on the previous page. Or, it could be done on top of a parachute while classmates create "waves." Another alternative would be to play water sound effects on a stereo, and spray the exposed puppeteers, as well as the audience, using a mist bottle. (Brown and Pleydell 1999, 87–99). Any of these options can create the desired story atmosphere better than a traditional puppet stage can.

Ingrid: In my professional life—both in the classroom and in performance—I seldom hide behind a puppet stage. By modeling puppet shows for students without using a stage, the children feel more comfortable performing shows in the open. Young children and puppet stages can be problematic in that children often forget to move the puppet because they are at a difficult angle to see the movement. I have no objection to people using a stage, but my personal preference is to use as few and simple stages as possible.

FIG 4-10 Plastic curtain as underwater puppet stage (scenery painted by Michele Valeri)

CHAPTER **5**

Puppets and Children with Special Needs

PUPPETS ARE EFFECTIVE in working with all children with unique needs, not just children in special education. This chapter addresses the use of puppets both in the special education classroom and in other early childhood classrooms. We will examine seven ways puppets can work for children with special needs. They include the following:

1. Children who are shy

2. Children diagnosed with attention deficit disorder or attention deficit hyperactivity disorder (ADD or ADHD)

3. Children with visual impairments

4. Children with hearing impairments

5. Children with autism spectrum disorders

6. Children who are developmentally delayed

7. Children with physical challenges

Ingrid: My friend's daughter attended the Maryland School for the Blind, and I was invited to do a puppet presentation in the multiply disabled program where the children were both blind and deaf. I was hesitant about the idea and wondered, "How do I perform for children who can't see or hear?" I knew that each child would be sitting with a sighted caregiver, so I decided to use a lesson that would be very tactile. I used a lion puppet with a removable mane, and told the story of how a lion grew his hair. The children laughed and giggled when the lion sat on their laps, and put one hand on the lion's mouth and the other on my neck to feel my larynx vibrate. The realization that I could communicate with a puppet and let the children learn about the puppet's personality was a revelation. I then designed shows for two kids at a time, letting them feel the moving puppets.

My work with the Maryland School for the Blind naturally segued into work with other groups with special needs. While I came into the field "through the back door," it became very clear to me that puppets are a powerful teaching tool for children who sometimes cannot be reached in other ways.

All of the lessons (except "The Wind") included in this book have been used in special needs classrooms. They were necessarily altered to make them developmentally appropriate.

Children Who Are Shy

Puppets are especially effective with children who are shy because they allow the child speaking through the puppet to communicate while "hiding" behind another persona. Children who may be unable to say something in front of the class may be able to take that risk if they feel it is the puppet taking the risk for them. Whether you manipulate the puppet or give it to the children, there is a basic protocol that should be followed when dealing with children who are shy.

First, enable rather than label. Calling a child shy may contribute to low self-esteem. If the teacher says in front of the class, "Oh, she won't do that because she's shy," the child may feel that she can't do what is expected in a self-fulfilling prophecy. Further, that sentiment may give her the perfect excuse for not trying because she is shy. Rather than being labeled, children should be given the opportunity to participate as they wish. Children should get the message that they may say either yes or no without any negative consequences for their choices. You should assure each child that she will be asked again, and that she can always change her mind. Don't stop asking a child to participate after being rebuffed the first several times, fearing that the child will only say "no" again. Make sure that your puppet protocol includes asking every child to participate every time.

Second, avoid the "tree trap." In an effort to give the shy child an opportunity to participate, you may be tempted to give the child the part of a prop or inanimate object. While having children play objects is a wonderful, creative way to involve them in the activity, it is counterproductive to consistently give that role to the child who is shy. Instead, offer her an active part in the same rotation as the other children. Try saying, "Sarah, would you like to be Mr. Bear today?" If the child shakes her head no, respond by saying, "That's okay. I'll ask you again later in case you change your mind." That offer should be made over and over again. Children who are considered shy are often disappointed in themselves for saying no and fear that they will never have another chance. Using the dialogue outlined above encourages the child who is shy to change his feelings of "I can't do it" to "I'm just not quite ready yet."

Third, children who are shy will pick up on the body language and subtle verbal nuances that give them the impression their teacher does not really expect them to participate. To avoid this, adopt a can-do attitude. Always expect in your heart that all of the children will participate.

Fourth, be consistent in using the same language with all of the children who do not participate. When children who typically participate refuse to, the same dialogue must be used for them as well as for the children who are shy. Children who find it difficult to participate should not feel that they are being singled out for different treatment.

Fifth, the children should feel as if "we're all in this together." Provide many opportunities for the children to do the same thing at the same time. Developmentally, there are benefits to having young children do a gesture, manipulate puppets, or chant a phrase together. When a child who is shy performs with the whole class, the transition to individual voluntary participation is easier. Sometimes shy children will do a gesture as asked but will do it in a small way. Teachers should pay attention for this, but not necessarily draw uncomfortable attention to the child with praise.

The point of this protocol is to create a comfortable, secure atmosphere where each child knows his choices will be respected. Creating this atmosphere requires patience and thought. The outcome, however, is most gratifying.

Children with Attention Deficits

All puppet lessons can easily be adapted for children with attention deficits. These changes are made by limiting or controlling three factors: time, stimuli, and space.

Time

An effort must be made to ensure that students with Attention Deficit Disorder or Attention Deficit Hyperactivity Disorder (ADD/ADHD) are only asked to wait an appropriate amount of time for their turn at manipulating a puppet. Do this by using lessons that allow all of the children to play a given part or manipulate a puppet simultaneously. In other words, if the lesson is one on pond life, instead of giving one group of children frog puppets, one group dragonfly puppets, and one group snake puppets, expecting each group to wait while the other demonstrates, create enough puppets so that everyone can first be a frog, then a dragonfly, then a snake over a number of days. This may mean that instead of purchasing a more expensive collection of pond animals, you will ask each child to create a simple stick puppet.

There is a trade-off in this scenario. While the lesson requires more preparation time on the part of the children, on the other hand, they will get the benefits of making their own puppets (for example, practice with fine motor skills, experience with creative representation, or a sense of ownership about the puppet). Also, the lesson is more likely to be successful for the children with attention deficits and therefore the whole class.

Teachers who have worked with children who have ADD/ADHD are familiar with the need to shorten lessons, or break them into parts, making it easier to attend and process. Activities and lessons featuring puppets are no different and in fact lend themselves to this kind of alteration. For example, when doing a long story like *Ducky*, you can increase the amount of sensory exposure to better hold the children's attention. Water may be represented with a parachute, spray bottles, or shower curtains. This necessitates doing the story over several days to keep each session from becoming too long and unmanageable. While *Ducky* may feasibly be done in one session with few props and supporting activities, it is more difficult for those with ADD to attend to. Adding sensory stimuli increases all young children's ability to attend to the lesson, especially children with ADD.

Stimuli

The element of stimuli usually refers to puppets themselves, but may include other factors as well. Certainly, flying a butterfly puppet around the room can be much more stimulating than sitting in a circle and manipulating the puppet. Again, there may be a trade-off: over-stimulation versus a physical outlet. There are a few suggestions, however, to help control stimuli in any situation. First, introduce the puppets through a graduated series of experiences designed to give the child incremental stimuli, rather than too much too soon. For example, if you are using butterfly puppets, first ask the children to use their hands to create butterfly wings. The children can review the movement vocabulary that will be available to them (*flutter, flit, soar, high, low, under,* and so on).

Classroom management can also be introduced, allowing the children to fly their hands near a classmate without touching. This also gives you the opportunity to demonstrate control devices, such as "butterfly napping" (the children put their hands on the floor). After the children have mastered flying techniques with their hands, the additional stimulus of using a puppet is not as overwhelming. Once the puppets repeat all of the actions and techniques done with the butterfly hands, more stimulating activities can be added, like flying around the room. Through this process, the children realize that the puppets have a specific use at any given time. The overall effect is to introduce stimulating elements in small amounts in order to let the children build to a more demanding activity without losing control of the class. This incremental stimulation should be repeated over several days so that participation is strengthened by motor memory.

The second point in dealing with stimulus is to never hand puppets to children who are not going to use them immediately. For example, if you are going to hand out eighteen puppets, don't hand them out one at a time. By the time the eighteenth child has received his puppet, the first child may be misusing hers. There are two ways to avoid this mistake. One, as you hand out the puppets, give the children something specific to do: "Make your puppet fly as high as you

Ingrid: In a class of children with developmental delays, several of which had ADHD, I did a lesson based on The Very Clumsy Click Beetle *by Eric Carle. The children made noises, and gestured to imitate characters and things in the book as I took them on a picture walk. Later, the teacher told me that the school's librarian had read the book to the children after I had. The poor librarian never had much experience with young children and in previous attempts to read to young children she failed to engage them. She had not planned any student involvement while reading* The Very Clumsy Click Beetle, *but the children spontaneously used the gestures, noises, and phrases I had used the day before. It worked like a charm, and for the first time there were no behavior problems during reading time.*

Ingrid: I was doing The Gigantic Turnip *with a classroom of twenty-four children. I gave each child a puppet by adding far more characters than were in the book. I asked the entire class to stand and have their puppet pull on the gigantic turnip. I found out later that the teacher had ran to her supervisor and said, "This is going to be chaos! Too many kids doing too many things!" However, it turned out to be a great lesson because each child was engaged with her own puppet. The teacher loved the idea.*

can without standing up." The instructions can be changed after a few seconds to keep the children involved until the last puppet has been handed out. Two, let the children know there will be a signal to pick up their puppets. Working with an aide, lay the puppets in front of the children very quickly and then let the children pick them up at the same time and use them. Make sure the children have the immediate gratification of touching and using the puppet.

The third point is that stimuli can be increased as needed by making sure that all children are engaged throughout the activity. Just as when considering time use, you may choose to let all of the children be a character simultaneously. You might also decide to let a group of children, along with a teaching assistant, carry out the action while the rest carry out a supporting activity. When doing *A Mushroom in the Rain,* for example, half of the children can operate animal puppets while the rest of the class creates the scene by making a rain noise and gesture.

Fourth, think about which puppets are being used and gauge how they will stimulate the children. Brightly colored puppets with several textures and moving parts may better engage and focus children. In addition, the teacher may choose a rod puppet with an animated hand to ensure that children have both hands involved with the puppet.

Fifth, always introduce the puppet properly, administering the puppet pledge, allowing the child to experiment with appropriate ways to use the puppet, and making the rules clear for what is acceptable and unacceptable when working with puppets. This is an important step any time puppets are used and it is especially important when working with children who have ADD/ADHD. In this introduction process the child should be acquainted with what will not be tolerated, but the emphasis should be on what is possible when operating the puppet, leaving the child with many ideas for creative outlets.

Space

Controlling the use of space is also easily done with puppets. If your class includes children who have trouble sitting in one place, give them a chance to move around the room. Invite them to use a large identified space with their puppets. The space may be identified in any number of ways, including tape on the floor, moving furniture to block off restricted areas, or a simple discussion and demonstration of spaces that are "out of bounds." When the butterfly flutters around the pond (see the sidebar), rather than flying the puppet while seated in a circle, students may be called on to fly to and from a prop flower. Or groups of children may be invited to move their butterflies around the room as long as they don't go into the art center. The teacher should plan the use of space carefully before the lesson begins, taking into account the element of time. While it may be advantageous to let the butterflies move in groups around the room, it may be difficult for some children to wait for their group's turn. Consider all three factors of time, space, and stimuli before deciding the best course of action.

You also can control space using props and imagination. For instance, blue fabric stretched out on the floor could represent a lake, or green fabric could be a meadow, or white cloth could become snow. This not only exercises the children's imagination but gives them a focal point.

Children with Visual Impairments

Teachers are often reluctant to use puppetry in a classroom that includes children with visual impairments. They see it as a visual art form. However, puppetry is also tactile and kinesthetic and can be successful with children who do not see well.

Exposed puppetry is a great technique for working with children with limited vision. It allows the children to feel, manipulate, and make friends with the puppets. When you are the puppeteer, the puppets should be introduced to small groups of two to four children. The same guidelines apply for proper introduction of a puppet, but then follow by making a short presentation with the puppets while allowing the children to feel the puppets. You might have to do several brief puppet presentations rather than one longer one in order to include all of the children in the classroom.

Similarly, when children with low or no vision manipulate the puppets themselves, try having them work in pairs. Each child can manipulate a puppet with one hand, freeing the other to feel the movement of his partner's puppet. This kind of activity works best in a small group format or with puppets in your learning centers. A puppet presentation

Ingrid: I was once working in a class with eighteen rambunctious boys. When I pulled out the butterfly puppets with 18-inch sticks, the teacher was more than skeptical. I was careful to let the children first act out butterflies with their hands, give the boys something to do with the puppets as soon as I handed them out, administer the puppet pledge (page 36) promising appropriate behavior while holding the butterflies, define the space by putting out flowers and grass for the boys to fly to, and give them directions as they flew to provide management. None of the sticks were used as weapons.

Ingrid: I volunteered in a number of classrooms at the Maryland School for the Blind, and the children and I had a wonderful time working together. I discovered that the best way for me to use the puppets was to have two children actually sit in my lap to feel the puppets while I did the presentation.

In contrast with that experience, I was once in a general education classroom that included a child who was blind. He did not like to be singled out, and did not want special attention. When I asked if he would like to feel the puppets, he always said no. Only when the entire class was invited to touch the puppet did he enthusiastically participate.

involving a few children can be successful if you choreograph the puppet-child placement. As with other children, puppet "shows" left to chance are both developmentally inappropriate and not enjoyable for anyone involved.

As with all children, the choice of puppet is key for the child with visual impairments. A puppet featuring a picture drawn on a piece of paper and taped to a stick might be fine in most circumstances; however, it would not be stimulating for children who can't see. Instead, give serious thought to the texture of the puppet and how it represents the character intended. For example, it is not unusual to find furry alligators for sale. While the teacher might buy such a puppet and then discuss the differences between puppet alligators and real alligators, another option is to buy or make a puppet that features a "scaly" fabric.

Other lessons with puppets are easily adapted too. These include activities that support emergent literacy skills using Braille word cards and children's books. Again, these are best conducted with small groups, allowing the children to touch the words and puppets. Lessons that use puppets to create original stories also work well with children who are visually impaired. However, they must be able to feel the difference between the characters.

Children with Hearing Impairments

Like most children, children with hearing impairments love puppets. Children who are Deaf in an otherwise hearing classroom should not be treated as special or different. For example, all children should have the same puppet, and all sign (and say) refrains. Like ESL speakers, these children often speak and understand a different language. The language they have in common with hearing populations is body language, filled with gestures and facial expressions. Puppets, however, have no facial expressions and children cannot read their lips. Therefore, to include children who are Deaf in puppet lessons, the material chosen should have certain qualities, including the following:

- Stories or activities that provide opportunities for action

- Opportunities for pantomime

- Simple language use allowing children to sign along, much like children who can hear might chant a repetitive phrase

In addition to all of these qualities, the attributes that make a particular book or activity appropriate for hearing children also are relevant here.

After selecting the material to be used, think carefully about the type of puppet and the space to be used. In the first category, you might be using an interpreter, in which case any developmentally appropriate puppet works well. If the lesson requires that the puppet sign, there are two types of puppets that have the necessary manual dexterity: the hat puppet and hand puppets with two gloved hands for use by either one or two puppeteers. Because gloved puppets may be prohibitive in terms of both creation and money, many teachers find hat puppets to be convenient and inexpensive.

Paint supply stores or hardware stores often have free painters' hats that can be turned into puppets. Baseball hats also work well for this purpose. When making a hat puppet, the eyes, nose, and ears are the most important features to be included. The mouth is of less importance. If you do not sign, the interpreter should wear the puppet hat, bobbing her head while signing for the character. The teacher then interprets for the hearing children. When this approach is taken, you and the interpreter must work closely together, planning the activity in advance. When selecting a space for the puppet lesson, exposed puppetry is better than a stage, so that all participants have visual contact with one another.

Children with Autism Spectrum Disorders

Puppets are particularly effective in working with children who have autism spectrum disorders because puppets are animated and can communicate, but they are not people and do not have human faces. One theory to explain the success of puppets in this context is that the human face gives off so many signals and facial expressions that being face-to-face with a human can be overwhelming, confusing, and frustrating for children who are unable to process the facial expressions.

Ingrid: One of the first activities I developed for children who are Deaf was with a circus theme. I knew only a few signs, and I had no interpreter. I had been advised to use loud marching music with a steady beat. After I started the march, I performed a pantomime circus with simple puppets doing silly cartoonlike tricks. I used a lot of slapstick with puppets falling down and fainting, and the puppets bowed after every trick. I didn't use a stage so everyone could see me; I used my facial expressions to enhance tension, showing concern for potentially injured puppets, and to express relief when they turned out to be okay. I even patted puppets on the back to congratulate them. The class loved the puppet show. Afterward, I asked them to make up puppet tricks and, to my surprise, they were amazingly inventive. Since then, I've done pantomime puppet circuses with all age groups and many different language speakers. It is always a big hit.

Puppets are nonthreatening in this way because there are fewer signals to indicate emotion.

Many of the same techniques mentioned throughout this text can also be applied to children with autism spectrum disorder (ASD). Once again, control of time, space, and stimuli is key. Layering and repeating activities and experiences is also a powerful tool for teachers, as many children with ASD have developmental skills that can fade and reappear. The same choices listed above with regard to these elements can be applied. Certainly, the protocol for children who are shy should be followed diligently. You should always include every child, never force a child to participate, offer each child a part every time even if there has been no interest in the past, and believe each and every time that the child will attend and participate at some point.

Ingrid: I was working with a child who displayed extreme autistic symptoms, was nonverbal, and did not participate in group settings. During my first five sessions he sat in the corner and didn't seem to notice I was there. Amazingly, before the fifth session he dragged his chair over to the circle, sat down, and buckled his seat belt! He continued to sit with us during each session for thirty minutes, which was a real accomplishment.

Another time, I was working with a classroom of three children on the autism continuum. One boy had lined up all the transportation toys in the classroom sorted by type: cars, trucks, airplanes, and motorcycles. The teacher asked me to see if he would break this rigid classification if a puppet asked him. I used a dog puppet named Fred that said, "I want to eat orange. Orange tastes so good. Do you have anything orange for me to eat?" At first the boy only gave Fred the orange cars, but with some coaxing from the puppet, he was able to pick out the other orange vehicles too. Then the puppet said, "Oh, no! I'm still hungry, and there are no more orange toys left. Now I want to eat red toys. Can you feed me the red ones?" He did beautifully with the activity, and really seemed to enjoy feeding the puppet. The teacher said that she had never been able to get this child to change classification midactivity and was amazed that the puppet could help him change the pattern.

The most successful work done with puppets and children with extreme autistic involvement is on a case-by-case basis. The teacher who knows the child well is the best one to decide when puppets are appropriate, what kind of puppet would be most appropriate, and how it will be presented to the child. It is not prudent to simply alter a standing lesson for children with severe developmental delays or ASD. Instead, a more relaxed, informal, improvised format is advised. Rather than using puppets during large group or small group time, go around to each child, working individually with him for as long as is comfortable, rarely for more than ten minutes. As with other students, selecting the right puppet is important, so a different puppet may be used for each child in this case. The content of the lesson should be tailored to the needs of the particular student. For example, if a child seems more alert and engaged when the classroom's pet rabbit is out of its cage, then you might choose a rabbit puppet or let the puppet discuss rabbits. Another child may respond favorably to tactile stimulus. In this case, you could stimulate the child by moving a furry mouse puppet up and down the child's arm while saying the first line of the nursery rhyme, "Hickory Dickory Dock, the mouse ran up the clock." To review body parts in this same situation, the mouse puppet could then run up the child's arm, head, or chest.

Children with Developmental Delays

Again, the tools used to adapt lessons for the other children outlined in the chapter are applicable to children with developmental delays. Issues of time, space, and stimuli should be addressed and the protocol for children who are shy should be used. Children who respond well to aural or visual cues might benefit from some of the suggestions for children who are visually and hearing impaired, such as use of puppets with texture or stories with a lot of action and pantomime. Similarly, the individual approach necessary for children with autism spectrum disorder can also be applied with developmentally delayed children. One other resource that has been successful with puppets is the use of adaptive technology. For example, children who are unable to speak for their puppets may be able to use a vocal augmentation device instead.

Ingrid: I was in a special education classroom in which they used model students from outside their student body. After a few sessions I asked if Penny was a model. The teacher was really pleased when she told me that Penny had Asperger's syndrome, a type of autism. She was bright and capable cognitively, but didn't interact with the other students or participate in group time. Working with the puppets allowed Penny to fully participate as a member of the class. The teacher had noticed Penny's reaction to the puppets, but was happy when I couldn't tell that she had Asperger's syndrome. It meant that Penny was so engaged with the activity that I couldn't even tell that she had the syndrome.

Children who have unintelligible speech should be included in these activities regardless of their verbal capabilities. When given a line such as, "Make your puppet say hello," the child's version of the word may not be understood in other situations; however, when using a puppet in the context of a known story, the intentions are clear.

Children with Physical Challenges

Any part of the body that can be moved can manipulate a puppet. For example, the head can operate a hat puppet. Whole wheelchairs can be turned into puppets by covering them with ponchos. Velcro fasteners can be used to attach puppets to feet, toes, elbows, or wrists. Puppets motivate children to move, and therefore can be used for incentive. They also can be used to vary the stimulus associated with exercise. For instance, the child who is encouraged to hold his head up for a short period of time is more interested in cooperating if it means he is manipulating his hat puppet during physical therapy.

Ingrid: Two exceptional teachers of children with developmental delays used technology to create an extremely successful lesson based on the book, Polar Bear, Polar Bear What Do You Hear? *They made foam puppets for each of the animals in the book, then recorded the appropriate animal noises on a vocal augmentation device. Students were able to make their puppets both move and speak.*

Ingrid: I use a puppet cheerleader often with children who use a walker. The puppet asks the child to take five steps. With each step the puppet cheers on the child, saying things like, "Wow! That was a good step!" and "You're almost there!"

CHAPTER 6

Puppet Lessons: Plans and Suggestions

THE LESSON PLANS included in this chapter are suggestions to give a general idea of what could be presented and to inspire further ideas. Avoid memorizing them or following them exactly; rather, feel free to practice and alter them to suit your needs.

The lessons are designed for large or small groups. They can typically be done with different puppets than those suggested and with other stories. Practice the activities in front of a mirror or with a volunteer, just as you would anytime you use a puppet. If you feel particularly nervous or if the lesson isn't a good fit for your skills or teaching goals, consider using a different lesson. Puppets are tools to bring variety, fun, and adventure to the learning process. If you have misgivings about particular puppet activities, then the point of using them is arguable. If this is the case, choose another activity, or devise your own activities and lessons to suit your personality and needs in the classroom.

Just as it is crucial for you to feel comfortable and confident in using puppets, it is equally important that the children are comfortable and confident in manipulating the puppets and in understanding the story or activity content. There are several good ways you can ensure this level of comfort:

- Familiarize the children with the story to be presented. You might read the story, tell the story, do a picture walk with the book (see page 70), present a puppet show with the children as a participating audience, or tell the story using gestures and visual cues that the children can imitate to help them remember the characters, sequence, and plot. The latter strategy works well with books or stories that feature several action verbs. An important caution if you choose to read the story first: do not try to use a puppet and hold the book at the same time. It is distracting to the children, and awkward for you.

- Make sure the puppets are introduced properly, giving the children an opportunity to manipulate them before starting the activity.

- Invite the children into the pretending. This means giving the children the opportunity to explore the movement possibilities with their puppet, speak for it in a typical and limited way, and establish the characteristics of the puppet that will later be expanded during the lesson. For example, before doing a lesson based on *Small Brown Dog's Bad Remembering Day,* which is included in this chapter, have the children pet their puppets, wag their puppet dog tails, bark, and give puppy kisses.

Once the book or story is selected and introduced to the children, choose a drama technique to present the story. Drama techniques to be considered include the following:

- The children act out the story with their bodies.

- All of the children play the main character simultaneously, and you play the other characters in person or with a puppet.

- You play the main character as a person or with a puppet; the children play the other characters.

In addition to selecting a drama technique, select a type of puppet to use: rod puppets, finger puppets, hand puppets, and so forth. Once this is done, the drama technique and optional picture walk should be reviewed to note how the action verbs will be carried out by the specific puppet. If necessary, new gestures may be devised to compensate for a puppet's limitations.

Lessons Based on Picture Books

Picture books are an excellent source for lesson material featuring puppets. Reading a book and then acting it out with puppets is an engaging way to provide children with the repetition they need to learn best. Many teachers have favorite books for use in a given unit. Adding puppets to the story gives the lesson another dimension. Furthermore, children who have strong visual intelligence may be stimulated by the pictures in the book, while children with kinesthetic or spatial intelligence may be best stimulated by a puppet re-creation of the book.

When selecting material for a lesson plan, whether using a picture book or some other source, a plot is unnecessary for a successful lesson. Often a list of related items serves as strong material for the preschool classroom (for example, *The Farmer in the Dell,* Molly Bang's *10, 9, 8,* or alphabet books). Similarly useful teaching tools include role plays that present a particular character, even though they may not include a plot.

As with other lessons for early childhood, some picture books are more appropriate for use in puppet lessons than others. Here are some things to look for when choosing a book to adapt to a puppet lesson:

- Repeated phrases

- A sense of humor that the children will appreciate

- A story that may involve travel

Ingrid: When I do a picture walk, sometimes the book actually becomes a puppet. This is demonstrated best in the lesson "Ducky." The book becomes a bird when I turn it over and flap the covers up and down. It becomes the boat by holding it in a V shape, and moving it as if it were floating on water.

- Opportunities for movement in puppet plays

- Inspiring pictures

- An element of surprise

- Characters that are animals or children

- An interesting atmosphere or setting

- The possibility for all of the children to be the main character

- A series of people or items that lend themselves to sequencing or simple math activities

- A plot that promotes problem-solving opportunities

While you won't find a book with all of these qualities, it is important to think about how the book will be used and which of the qualities listed above is most critical to support the curricular goal being presented. If a book you choose is too long, it can be edited simply by skipping pages. If the story would work well in the lesson but the language is developmentally inappropriate, tell the story in your own words rather than read it. If it is otherwise good for use in this context but is for more mature children, a "picture walk" using just the illustrations while paraphrasing the text for young children is in order.

Doing a Picture Walk

Some advance preparation and thought should be put into developing a picture walk. Following the steps below will help you prepare:

- It is especially important to read the book several times until it is familiar. Efforts to have the children sequence the events in the story will be unsuccessful if you are unfamiliar with the sequence yourself. Examine the story carefully to decide if there are sections that are not active, are confusing, or are not essential to the story being told. Alter or omit these sections.

- Practice telling the story as it will be told on the picture walk. The text will not be read verbatim. Rather, this will be a unique, perhaps summarized, interpretation of the plot. If the picture walk varies from the actual text, you can read the book later and ask the children to identify the differences.

- Become familiar with all of the pictures. Devise questions to ask the children that can be answered based on the illustrations and that will help confirm their understanding of the plot. Anticipate confusion about illustrations or a literal interpretation of the pictures.

- Identify or create repetitive phrases. The children may repeat these phrases as the story is being told. A hand gesture should be created to help remind students of the phrase and to help cue the children so they know when to repeat it.

- Identify the action verbs in the story and invent hand gestures for the students to use when they hear them.

- If a book is otherwise good for use in this context but does not contain the language you are trying to encourage, include your own words in the picture walk. Children can use the new language with their puppets when acting out the story.

When developing a picture walk, it is not necessary to closely adhere to the book. Introducing a new author's work shows an appreciation for the writer that the children will internalize. Demonstrating how the book can be presented in a variety of ways encourages young children to use their own imaginations to bring books alive in the classroom.

The question of whether to read the book before or after puppets present the lesson must be answered on a case-by-case basis. When you change the story, it is best to read the book afterward, asking the children to identify the things that were altered. This becomes a compare-and-contrast exercise. If the intent is to emphasize concepts about the story or sequencing, it is a good idea to read the book first, asking the children to recall the story and its order while enacting it with puppets.

Ingrid: I first heard the Ask Mr. Bear *story from my friend and colleague Dr. Victoria Brown before I ever saw the book. I began using it as a puppet show plot, and really made it my own. When the book was republished, I was delighted to have the book available for the children, but realized I liked the flexibility of my own version and wanted to continue to present it. Many times in a college setting I'll present this story with my own zoo animal puppets. Then I'll bring out a box of purchased farm animal puppets and ask the students to create their own puppet presentation using the new characters and based on what they saw me do. The students are always surprised to find out how successful and creative they can be with their alterations.*

Jamal and Mr. Bear
(Inspired by *Ask Mr. Bear*)

FIG 6-1 Cast of characters for "Jamal and Mr. Bear" (Zebra, Mr. Bear, Monkey, Mama Giraffe, Jamal, and Elephant). Instructions for puppets are on pages 159–161.

Basis for lesson

Ask Mr. Bear, by Marjorie Flack

Puppet use

Puppet telling a story

Character types

Animals

Drama techniques

Read the book after puppet presentation (page 69), age-appropriate presentation by children (page 23), adapting a story structure (page 33).

Content

This lesson works well in observance of Mother's Day, Father's Day, or any other event where gifts are traditionally given. It can be used to review order and sequencing by asking questions such as, "Who did Jamal ask first?" It may be included to review or introduce animal identification.

Method 1

The basic plot from *Ask Mr. Bear* is adapted to meet the curricular goals of the teacher. The bear character remains, but the rest of the plot is carried out by farm animals, zoo animals, or people, as desired. Half of the class presents the story while the other half acts as an "audience." The story is presented again with the performers now being the audience. This method is most appropriate for more mature children. You will need enough puppets for half the class.

Method 2

Again, the characters may be altered, with the exception of the bear. The story is divided into scenes with two characters in each scene. A different child manipulates the main character each time, along with each new puppeteer or character that is introduced. The performance is only done once as all of the children will have a chance to use a puppet character. This method is appropriate for children who are capable of briefly waiting for a turn and using the puppet independently. You will need enough puppets for half of the class (half of the children will play Jamal or the main character).

Method 3

All students play the main character, and the teacher acts as the other parts. This method is appropriate for young children and children who have speech delays. You will need enough Jamal or main character puppets for the entire class.

Materials needed for methods 1 & 2

Enough puppets for half of the class, including the main character, a mother, and a bear.

Materials needed for method 3

Enough main character puppets for each child, and a bear puppet, mother puppet, and other puppets for the teacher.

Preparation

1) Create or purchase a toy, a bear, a main character, a mother, and other puppets as needed.

2) Decide which holiday to highlight in the story (for example, Mother's Day, a birthday, Valentine's Day, and so forth).

3) Run through the lesson without the children.

4) Seat the children in a semicircle.

5) Act out the entire story for the students, breaking it down into scenes. Use a puppet in each hand, changing the puppets between scenes.

SCENE 1: JAMAL THE GIRAFFE

Teacher as Jamal:	(*speaking to audience*)
	Hi! I'm Jamal the Baby Giraffe. I have a big problem. Mother's Day is soon and I don't know what to get my mommy. I'm going to ask some of my friends at the zoo if they have any ideas. I think I'll ask the elephant first. (*calling out*) Oh, Mrs. Elllllephaaaant!

SCENE 2: JAMAL AND MRS. ELEPHANT

Teacher as Mrs. E:	Yyyyeees?
Teacher as Jamal:	I need a present for my mommy for Mother's Day. What can I give her?
Teacher as Mrs. E:	Why don't you give her some peanuts?
Teacher as Jamal:	Noooooo, my mommy doesn't like to eat peanuts. She likes to eat leaves.
Teacher as Mrs. E:	You really should ask Mr. Bear. He's the smartest animal in the zoo.
Teacher as Jamal:	NO! I'm scared of Mr. Bear. I'll go ask Mr. Zebra. (*calling*) Oh, Mr. Zeeebra!

SCENE 3: JAMAL AND MR. ZEBRA

Teacher as Mr. Z:	(*bleating words*) Yeeeeeeees?
Teacher as Jamal:	I need a present for my mommy for Mother's Day. What can I give her?
Teacher as Mr. Z:	Why don't you give her some hay?
Teacher as Jamal:	Nooooooo, my mommy doesn't eat hay. She eats leaves.
Teacher as Mr. Z:	Well then, you'll have to ask Mr. Bear. He's the smartest animal in the zoo.
Teacher as Jamal:	NO! I'm scared of Mr. Bear.
Teacher as Mr. Z:	I guess I can't help you then.
Teacher as Jamal:	I'll go ask the monkey. (*calling*) Oh, Monkeeeeeeey!

SCENE 4: JAMAL AND MR. MONKEY

Teacher as Monkey:	*(bouncing up and down)* What! What! What! What!
Teacher as Jamal:	I need a present for my mommy for Mother's Day. What can I give her?
Teacher as Monkey:	*(bouncing up and down)* Bananas, bananas, bananas!
Teacher as Jamal:	Nooooooo, my mommy doesn't eat bananas. She eats leaves.
Teacher as Monkey:	*(bouncing up and down)* Ask the Bear! Ask the Bear! Ask the Bear! He's smart.
Teacher as Jamal:	NO! I'm scared of Mr. Bear.
Teacher as Monkey:	Too bad. Good-bye.
Teacher as Jamal:	*(to audience)* Should I ask Mr. Bear? I'm so scared of him. *(audience volunteers "Yes!")*

Other characters are added here depending on which puppets are available to the teacher.

SCENE 5: JAMAL AND MR. BEAR

Teacher as Jamal:	*(calling very quietly)* Mmmmm-mister Bbbbbb-beaaaar!
Teacher as Mr. Bear:	*(loudly)* WHAT!
Teacher as Jamal:	*(timidly, with a shaking voice)* I need a ppppppp-present for my mmmmm-mommy.
Teacher as Mr. Bear:	*(loudly)* Come closer!
Teacher as Jamal:	*(timidly, with a shaking voice)* Is this close enough?
Teacher as Mr. Bear:	*(loudly)* No, closer!
Teacher as Jamal:	*(timidly, with a higher shaking voice)* Is this close enough?
Teacher as Mr. Bear:	*(loudly)* No, closer!
Teacher as Jamal:	*(timidly, with an even higher shaking voice)* Is this close enough?
Teacher as Teacher:	*(to the audience, demonstrating with puppets)* Then Mr. Bear gave Jamal a great big bear hug.
Teacher as Mr. Bear:	*(loudly)* Give that to your mom. She'll like that.

Teacher:	*(to the audience)* Jamal was so excited he ran all the way home, saying:
Teacher as Jamal:	Mommy! Mommy! Mommy! Mommy!

SCENE 6: JAMAL AND MOMMY

Teacher as Jamal:	Mommy, I have a present for you.
Teacher as Mommy:	What is it, Dear?
Teacher as Jamal:	You have to come closer!
Teacher as Mommy:	Is this close enough?
Teacher as Jamal:	No, closer!
Teacher as Mommy:	Is this close enough?
Teacher as Jamal:	No, closer!
Teacher as Mommy:	Is this close enough?
Teacher as Jamal:	Yes!
Teacher:	*(to the audience, demonstrating with puppets)* Then Jamal gave his mommy a great big bear hug.
Teacher as Mommy:	That's the best present you could have given me! *(kisses Jamal loudly and repeatedly)*

Lesson with suggested dialogue

Method 1

Using Jamal the Giraffe and zoo animals on Mother's Day

Teacher to class:	I'm glad you liked that story. I had a good time doing it for you. I thought that you would have a good time doing this puppet show too.
	Choose a child to play the main character. Briefly put the puppet in the child's hand and let him make the puppet wave to the rest of the class to establish appropriate puppet manipulation.
Teacher to child:	Okay, now make Jamal say, "I need a present for my mommy on Mother's Day."
	Child repeats the sentence as he is able.
Teacher to child:	Now Jamal says, "I'll ask my friends for ideas."
	Child repeats the sentence as he is able.

Teacher to class:	Class, raise your hand if you know who Jamal went to first?
Children respond until they come up with the correct answer.	
Teacher:	That's right, an elephant! Cory, would you like to be the elephant? Good, come up here, and put out both hands. Hold this stick in this hand, and this stick in the other hand. Now make the elephant wave and say hello. Good.
Now go back to the child playing Jamal and speak to the puppet.	
Teacher to puppet:	Jamal, say, "What can I get my mommy for Mother's Day?"
Child repeats the sentence as he is able.	
Teacher to puppet:	Mrs. Elephant, say, "Give her peanuts."
Child repeats the sentence as she is able. The child playing Jamal may respond no or say, "No, Mommy doesn't like peanuts," *having already seen the play. If not, the child should be prompted. If so, the teacher prompts the elephant.*	
Teacher to puppet:	Make the elephant say, "Ask Mr. Bear. He's the smartest animal in the zoo."
Child repeats the sentence as she is able.	

Continue to prompt the puppeteers as needed. The child playing Jamal remains on "stage" and another child is chosen to play the next animal introduced in the story. Only those operating puppets should be holding them. Use as much language as the children can process. The story is repeated, using as many characters as necessary until half of the class has had an opportunity to be a puppeteer. Allow puppeteers to bow and the audience to clap for them. Then reverse roles and do the story again. Because these students have just seen the story performed, they will need less prompting and assistance.

Method 2

Follow Method 1, prompting children with the lines as needed. The parts of both Jamal and the other characters are rotated to a different child each time a scene changes. Additional characters are added to accommodate the entire class. For instance, a lion, an alligator, and a jaguar can be included. Simplify the language to meet the students' abilities by asking them to repeat the sentences using shorter phrases, such as

> Make the Elephant say, "Ask Mr. Bear. He's the smartest."

Method 3

Hand out a Jamal puppet to each child, showing how to hold it appropriately. Adult aides may assist in this process.

Teacher to class: Now make Jamal wave. All you Jamals, say hello. Now say, "I need a present."

Children repeat the phrase as a group.

Teacher: "For my mommy."

Children repeat the phrase as a group.

Teacher: Now say, "I'll ask the elephant."

Children repeat the sentence as a group. Pick up the elephant puppet.

Teacher: Jamals, say, "What can I get my mommy?"

Children repeat the sentence as a group. Operate the elephant to respond.

Teacher as Mrs. Elephant: Give her peanuts. She'll like that!

The children playing Jamal may respond with no, or "No, Mommy doesn't like peanuts," having already seen the play. If not, they should be prompted. If so, the teacher operates the elephant.

Teacher as Mrs. Elephant: Then go ask Mr. Bear. He's the smartest animal in the zoo.

Teacher to class: Make Jamal say, "No, I'm scared of Mr. Bear."

Continue the story as indicated until Jamal goes to see Mr. Bear.

Teacher to class: Jamals, say "Mmmmm-Mr. Bbbbb-Bear."

Children repeat the sentence as a group. Hold up the bear puppet.

Teacher as Mr. Bear: WHAT?

Teacher to class: Jamals, say, "I need a pppp-present . . ."

Children repeat the phrase as a group.

Teacher to class:	Say, "For my mmmm-mommy."

Children repeat the phrase as a group.

Teacher as Mr. Bear:	Come closer!
Teacher to class:	Stop!

The children must be stopped at one or two steps. The children step forward and say, "Is this close enough?"

Teacher as Mr. Bear:	(louder) No! Come closer!
Teacher to class:	Stop!

The children step forward and say, "Is this close enough?"

Teacher as Mr. Bear:	(even louder) NO, CLOSER!
Teacher to class:	STOP!

Repeat the process until all of the children are huddled around the bear puppet.

Teacher as Mr. Bear:	YES! (hugging each puppet) Give this to your mother.

The children remain standing.

Teacher:	Then all the Jamals ran home. Can you make your puppet run by bouncing it in place like Shauna's puppet?

Bring out the mommy puppet.

Teacher to class:	Say, "Mommy, I have a present for you."
Teacher as Mommy:	What is it, Jamal?
Teacher to class:	Jamals, what do you have for your mommy?
Children:	A hug!

The Mommy puppet hugs each Jamal, then the puppets are collected and the children sit down.

Ducky

FIG 6-2 Cast of characters from "Ducky" (Frog, Duck, Turtle, and Beaver). Instructions for puppets are on pages 162–169.

Basis for lesson

Ducky, written by Eve Bunting and illustrated by David Wisniewski

Puppet use

Specialty puppet, puppet actors

Character types

Inanimate objects

Drama techniques

Story done in a series of sessions (page 56), picture walk (page 68), animating the book (page 68), using props for sensory stimulus (page 57), creating story atmosphere (page 51).

Content

This activity is appropriate for units on ocean life and supports the concepts of sink and float, story sequence, middle and end. It also assists in teaching the colors yellow, blue, green, and red.

Materials

Parachute, toy boat, small brown box, duck, beaver, frog, and turtle puppets (every class member should have one bath toy puppet), one green snake puppet, one shark puppet, pelican paper puppet (optionally, one for each class member), piece of bubble wrap approximately 18 by 24 inches or alternatively, bubble-blowing liquid and wand.

Preparation

1) Develop a picture walk through the book. Paraphrase the story appropriately for the developmental level of the class. Animate the book as you go along, flying the book and flapping its covers to imitate birds, sailing the book along as if it is a boat, and moving the book to imitate Ducky's adventures.

2) If the children do not know what a beaver is, use pictures, video, or a realistic toy to familiarize the children with real beavers. (Most children know ducks, turtles, and frogs and need little information on them for this story.)

3) Bring in a rubber ducky to help the children understand what the book is about.

4) Make duck, beaver, frog, turtle, and pelican puppets as described in chapter 7 or purchase the necessary puppets, or let the children make simple versions.

5) Practice the lesson without the children present.

Session 1

Beginning the lesson

Present a picture walk of *Ducky*. Put the book away. Have the children sit down around the parachute. If there are classroom rules for parachute use, review them before starting the activity. If this is the first time a parachute has been used, rules must be established. Spread out the parachute with the children sitting all around it, making sure that the parachute is not tight. Explain that they are not to sit on or under the parachute, but must remain seated at the edge of the parachute at all times. Tell the children that there are signals for using the parachute: "Parachute down," "Let go," and "Hands up." Demonstrate what the children are to do when they hear each of the signals. Guide the class to make big waves. After you put down the parachute and watch it settle, practice making waves and keeping the parachute still several times.

Let the children help create the atmosphere of the story by having them "dip their hands in the water" and "splash their faces." Have them hang on to the parachute and put their legs underneath. Let them kick to "get their legs wet" and make the parachute move.

Lesson with suggested dialogue

Teacher: Do you remember the book *Ducky?* It is the story of something that really happened. I want to use our imaginations and act out Ducky's story today. Do you remember what happens at the beginning of the book?

Let the children respond until they mention the boat or the storm or the box of bath toys.

Teacher: That's right! Ducky and his friends were in a box on a boat that was sailing on the ocean. The parachute is going to be our ocean.

Place the toy boat with a box on top of it in the middle of the parachute. Direct the children to make waves with the parachute, tossing the boat around until the box falls out of it.

Teacher: Ocean down. Let go. Hands up. Very good. Now, without making waves, can everyone lift the parachute high over your heads?

Put the ducks, frogs, beavers, and turtles under the parachute while explaining:

Teacher: When the storm tossed the box out, it sank to the bottom of the ocean. It broke open and all the toys came out of the box! Keep the ocean up high and when I call your name, you may dive under the water and help one of the bath toys float to the surface.

Call the children's names two to four at a time. The class continues to hold up the parachute while each child picks a toy and makes it float up from the bottom.

Teacher: Ocean down. Let go. Hands up. Very good. Now we're going to let our toys float on the wavy ocean. Put your toy in one hand, and use your other hand to make waves in the ocean. These toys sailed for days, and days, and days.

We're going to visit them tomorrow to find out what happens next. Now if you have a yellow duck, bring it to me and then go back and sit down.

Continue to collect animals in this fashion.

Teacher: Now push the ocean as far as you can into the center of the circle.

Gather up the parachute for the next session.

Session 2

Beginning the lesson

Spread the children out in a circle around the parachute and review the rules of parachute use. Review the story thus far, showing the props from the last session as you talk about them. Keep one puppet for future activity modeling and pass the rest to the students.

Lesson with suggested dialogue

Teacher: Our toys have been floating for days, and they may float to different children today. You may have had a duck last time, and this time you might get a beaver.

Walk around the circle handing out the bath toy puppets. Have each child hold his or her toy on the waves, re-creating the last thing they did in session 1.

Teacher: Ocean up. Ocean down. Let go. Hands up. Now what came next in the story?

Let the children respond until a snake is mentioned. If no one remembers the snake, bring out the puppet as a cue for the children. Demonstrate with a toy how the snake puppet will play with it. Walk around on the parachute, slinking the snake around each of the children and their toys. Ask each child for permission before coming near them with the snake puppet.

Teacher:	This snake really likes playing with the ducks and the beavers and the frogs and the turtles. All right, what happens next?

Let the children respond until a shark is mentioned. In the unlikely event that no one remembers the shark, bring out the puppet as a cue for the children. Walk around on the parachute, tasting each of the bath toys and spitting it out in turn.

Teacher as Shark:	Pitoey!
Teacher:	You know, I think the shark is really hungry, but he doesn't like the taste of the toys.

In large classes or those that are prone to lack of control, use one paper pelican puppet. Fly it around in circles over the toys. The class can make the toy puppets say, "I wish I could fly," "I don't like this big ocean," or "I wish that pelican would take me flying."

In smaller classes or those with more mature children, the students can put their toys on the parachute and then each child is given a pelican puppet. The class stands up and "flies" over the toys and around the room looking at the sights. The children can make up lines like, "Look at the pretty toys" or "I think I see beavers in the ocean!" The class can fly over another part of the room and spy on the shark puppet. They can swoop down and grab an imaginary fish out of the ocean for dinner, then fly back around the parachute. Seat the children and collect the pelicans.

Teacher:	Pick up your toy again, put it on the ocean, and let's make some waves. Ocean up. Ocean down.

Let the children bounce their toys on the waves for a few seconds.

Teacher:	Ocean down. Hands up. Now if you have a yellow duck, bring it to me and then go back and sit down.

Continue to collect animals in this fashion.

Teacher:	Now push the ocean as far as you can into the center of the circle.

Gather up the parachute for the next session.

Session 3

Beginning the lesson

Spread the children out in a circle around the parachute and review the rules of parachute use. Review the story thus far, showing the props from the last session as you talk about them. When reviewing the shark, you may have him go around and taste the toys again, spitting each one out, "Pitoey."

Lesson with suggested dialogue

Teacher: After the pelicans flew away, a big storm blew in and tossed the toys in big waves. Can you help me make big waves?

Practice making waves with the children, then have them put the parachute down. Select two to six children to go into the center of the parachute with their puppets. Children holding the edge of the parachute may do so with one hand, allowing the other to bob their bath toy at the edge of the water.

Teacher: Now, toys in the ocean, let me see how you bounce way up and way down in the waves.

Let the children practice letting their toys ride the imaginary waves.

Teacher: Now we're ready to make waves for the toys to ride. Ocean up!

Repeat this process until all of the children have had an opportunity to float on the ocean in the middle of the parachute. [FIGURE 6-3] Another option is to take a puppet to the center of the parachute and let the children make waves.

Teacher: Finally the toys bumped into some rocks. Where were the rocks? What happened next?

Let the children respond until they mention how the children find the toys.

Teacher: How would you feel if you found a toy like that?

FIG 6-3 Valerie Bayne Carroll with a preschool class, making waves on the ocean with their "Ducky" puppets. Andrew Welch sits in the middle of the ocean parachute holding his beaver puppet.

Let the children respond while facilitating the use of language to describe emotions.

Teacher:

Let's act out the part where the children find the bath toys. Put your toy on the edge of the ocean. Now let's all stand up and turn around so you can't see the toy. Great. Now turn around and pretend you have just found a new toy. What will you say? What will your face look like?

While the children turn their backs to "find" their toys, pick up the parachute from the middle of the circle.

Teacher:

Okay, now that you've found a bath toy, I want to ask you about it. Please turn around and sit in the circle with your toy.

Ask each child a question about his or her toy. Vary the questions as you go around the circle.

| Teacher: | (to various children) What kind of toy did you find? What color is your bath toy? How did you feel when you found that toy? |

After asking each child a question, ask the group some questions to review the experience.

| Teacher: | (to various children) How did these toys feel about being in the ocean? What did the toys love? What did the boy and the ducky do at the end of the story? |

Let the children respond until the bath is mentioned. Go around the circle and gently wrap the bubble wrap around each puppet one at a time. Make bathing noises the children will enjoy.

| Teacher: | Scruba-dub-dub! Splish splash! Bubble, bubble, bubble! |

Alternatively, bubbles can be blown at each puppet while walking around the circle.

I Am Not a Dinosaur

Basis for lesson

I Am Not a Dinosaur, by Mary Packard and illustrated by Nate Evans

Puppet use

Specialty puppet, puppet actors

FIG 6-4 Michele Valeri hands a pterodactyl puppet to Katharine T. Manor.

Character type

Animals

Drama techniques

A puppet for each child (page 58), puppet presentation using entire classroom space (page 58), crossing the body midline

Content

I Am Not a Dinosaur can be used in units on dinosaurs to demonstrate sorting and classification, the scientific principle of perspective, and gliding versus flapping, and to introduce new vocabulary.

Materials

One paper pterodactyl puppet for each child, a mirror, large dinosaur models or pictures for those discussed in the book, small dinosaur toys, one large cutout of a dinosaur footprint, one large paper Mama Pterodactyl puppet.

Preparation

1) Make a pterodactyl puppet for each child plus a couple of extras in case one is torn. Create one larger Mama Pterodactyl puppet. Directions for these puppets are given on pages 170–171.

2) Read the book several times and decide which parts may be omitted.

3) Collect the props and pictures needed.

4) Practice the lesson without the children present.

Note

On the page headed "Fly Away," the author writes, "The animal in this story is not a dinosaur. It is a rhamphorynchus. It has wings and can fly, and is actually a bird." Scientists know that rhamphorynchus was not a bird because it had fur rather than feathers. In this lesson, the more familiar name, *pterodactyl,* is used rather than rhamphorynchus even though it is not scientifically correct. When using this lesson, be aware of the scientific basis for it, since some children are "experts" in prehistoric times.

Beginning the lesson

Arrange the children in a circle. As a class, put the dinosaurs around the room to create atmosphere. Use this opportunity to sort and classify the dinosaurs and discuss their various attributes. Look at the cover of the book with your students and study the creature. Discuss its body parts and relative sizes: Make sure to note the big head and small feet, as well as its tail, wings, feet, nose, arms, hands, and teeth. Discuss the teeth with the children. Note that flying reptiles were meat eaters. The smaller ones ate bugs and the larger ones ate fish. Point out that the wings of flying reptiles are actually an extension of one of their fingers, which grows very long and wide to form a wing.

Read *I Am Not a Dinosaur* and show the pictures to your students. Discuss each page in detail. Have the entire class repeat each sentence you read. On pages that do not have complete sentences, you may make sentences out of phrases in the book for the children to repeat; for example, "A longer neck" becomes "I wish I had a longer neck," and

"A special tail" becomes "I wish I had a special tail." Put the book away, and pass out the paper pterodactyl puppets and practice flying them. Show each child one at a time how to hold the puppet properly by placing it in the child's hands, then show how to flap the wings by gently moving the child's hands. The pterodactyl puppets are fragile, and this step is especially important for young children or children who have motor impairments.

Lesson with suggested dialogue

Teacher:	Now that everyone has a puppet and you've all practiced moving the wings on your own, let's try it together. Can you make your puppet fly high? Wow, Carmen is really reaching up high, and she's very gentle with her pterodactyl too. Can you make your puppet fly low? Jarred is doing a good job flying his pterodactyl down low without touching his neighbors. Pterodactyls can fly by flapping their wings like we are doing, or by gliding. Gliding means that the pterodactyl is letting the air hold him up. He lets the wind help him move from one place to another in the sky. Can you let your pterodactyls glide instead of flapping? I like the way Simone is letting her puppet soar and glide without moving its wings. Let's pretend that in the middle of our circle is a lake. Make your pterodactyl swoop down to the imaginary lake and catch a fish.

Pull the hand mirror out from a box, and move to each child around the circle.

Teacher:	I'm going to come around to each of you, and hold this mirror up to your pterodactyl. Is your pterodactyl a dinosaur? When I come around with the mirror, your pterodactyl can look in the mirror and say, "I am not a dinosaur!" Ready?

Let the children respond, reviewing the title of the book. After taking the mirror to each child, show the children a picture or plastic model of a triceratops.

| Teacher: | Do you remember this triceratops? Raise your hand if you can tell me what the pterodactyl said when he saw the triceratops. Have the children respond until one child mentions, "I don't have horns" or "I wish I had horns." |

Bring out other pictures (or models) and let the children remember what the pterodactyl said about each. It is not necessary for the children to remember the exact sentence from the book, as long as they remember the correct attribute the pterodactyl comments upon.

| Teacher: | Do you remember how the book ended? Raise your hand if you know what happened. |

Let the children respond. If they need help, ask guiding questions.

| Teacher: | Did the pterodactyl meet someone who was not a dinosaur? Did this animal look like him? What color was the animal? |

Once the children have discussed Mama, bring her out and speak for her, flapping her wings slightly.

| Teacher as Mama Pterodactyl: | "You know, little pterodactyl, having wings is best because even though dinosaurs are big, from up in the sky they look little!" |

Put the puppet down, and use your own voice.

| Teacher: | Everyone stand up and let Mama take the baby flying around in the sky. I'll take the Mama around the room, and you can fly your babies behind me. |

Pick up the Mama puppet.

| Teacher: | Let's go! Oh, look! There's a triceratops. See how small she looks from here? Fly right over her babies so you can see. That's a grown-up triceratops too. She just looks small because we're looking at her from way up here in the sky. It's getting hot. Let's get out of the sun and fly under a tree and rest. |

Concepts that are a part of other curriculum may also be included if desired, such as:

"Babies, this is an electrical outlet. Stay away from that! I don't want you to get hurt! Look, I see two red things down there. Babies, what do you see that is red?"

Continue to fly around the room until they've seen all of the dinosaurs that have been put out.

Teacher: My goodness, all that flying has made me hungry. Are you hungry too? Let's go to that lake over there, and swoop down to catch some more fish. Good. Has everyone gobbled down a fish? Let's stop on this cliff to rest for a moment. My wings are tired from all this flapping. Whew. Now it's time to fly back home. Are you ready?

Glide and flap back to the circle. Collect the puppets.

Small Brown Dog's Bad Remembering Day

Basis of lesson

Small Brown Dog's Bad Remembering Day, written by Mike Gibbie and illustrated by Barbara Nascimbeni

Character types

Animals

Puppet use

Specialty puppet, puppet actors

FIG 6-5 Cast of characters for "Small Brown Dog's Bad Remembering Day" (Back row: Sid, Tess, Bobby, Alf, Peaches, Ralph. Middle row: Patch, Dan. Front row: Charlie.) Instructions for puppets are on pages 172–176.

Drama techniques

Hand gestures before puppet presentation (page 69), creating story atmosphere (page 51), accommodating the developmental level of the class (page 30).

Content

This activity gives children practice reviewing concepts about story. It can be used in units on animals and pets and directional prepositions. Most other curriculum subjects can be included as desired.

Materials

One small brown dog puppet with a pink nose for each child participating, up to seven different dog puppets to represent characters in the story. Alternatively, dog puppets may be made from black tube socks as described in chapter 7. In this case, the reference should be to the "Small Black Dog" throughout the lesson.

Preparation

1) Develop a picture walk for *Small Brown Dog's Bad Remembering Day*. Note the action verbs used in the story: *scratch, dig, splash,* and so forth. Emphasize the dog's name, Patch. Based on the children's developmental maturity, decide if the teacher will tell the children what gestures to use to represent each verb, or if the children will be invited to create their own gestures to use as a group.

2) Make or purchase puppets for the story. Due to the many action verbs used in the story, spend extra time experimenting with the puppets to see what they are capable of.

3) Practice the lesson without the children present.

Lesson with suggested dialogue

Do a picture walk of *Small Brown Dog's Bad Remembering Day* with the children. Pause when you come to the first action verb, *wake*.

Teacher:	Look! The small brown dog with the pink nose wakes up! Can you raise your hand and show me how you wake up in the morning?

Let several children respond, acting out waking up.

Teacher:	Zana and Teddy opened their eyes and stretched their arms out. I think that is a good way to wake up. Let's all try that together.

Demonstrate the waking-up gesture with the class. Continue the picture walk through the book until Small Brown Dog looks around for his collar.

Teacher:	Uh-oh! Small Brown Dog can't find his collar. Look up. Is his collar there? Look down. Is his collar there?

Let the children move their heads up and down, and answer, yelling no, when asked if they see the collar. Continue with the picture walk, creating a gesture for each action verb. The language may be abbreviated to suit the developmental level of the classroom. For example, as Small Brown Dog meets other dogs, they may respond to him by saying, "No, I don't remember your name, but I do remember that you like to splash in puddles," rather than the longer dialogue used in the book.

You may choose to emphasize a particular key experience or curricular element by including it in Small Brown Dog's adventures. For example, when working on numbers, ask the children to splash, eat hot dogs, or dig up bones a certain number of times. If safety is an issue, have the children look both ways before crossing the street along with Small Brown Dog on the way to the police station. When Small Brown Dog finally retrieves his collar and reviews what he likes to do, this becomes a review of the lesson as well. Use the gestures as you look at the pictures and recount each of the action verbs. Ask the children why they think Small Brown Dog's name is Patch, and facilitate a discussion.

Teacher:	I like the story of Small Brown Dog with the pink nose. I think it would be exciting to act it out with puppets. Look what I have here! It is a small brown dog with a pink nose! I have a small brown dog for you, and a small brown dog for you . . .

Introduce the puppets to the children using the proper protocol. Invite the children into the pretending.

Teacher:	Okay, have your puppet wag its tail. Very good. Can your puppet drink from a bowl of imaginary water? Good! Now have Small Brown Dog give you a great big kiss. Sllllluuuurp. Oooooo! Gross! We better wipe that off. Do you remember how the story started? Small Brown Dog was asleep. Have Small Brown Dog lie down. Now Small Brown Dog wakes up. Ring-ring! It's the alarm clock. Wake up Small Brown Dog. Now make him say, "I can't remember my name."

The children repeat the phrase.

Teacher:	Look for his collar. Have your puppet look up; down; to the side; to the other side. Uh-oh, no collar. What does Small Brown Dog do first when he can't find his collar?

Let the children respond until one says that Small Brown Dog runs outside.

Teacher:	That's right! Have Small Brown Dog run outside like this. Stop! Small Brown Dog sees Tess the Terrier.

Pull out the Tess the Terrier puppet.

Teacher:	Say, "Help! Tess, I can't remember my name!"

The children repeat the phrase with their puppets. The teacher responds with the terrier puppet.

Teacher as Tess the Terrier:	I know you're a small brown dog with a pink nose, but I can't remember your name. But I do remember that you like to splash in puddles.

Teacher:	Make Small Brown Dog say, "You're right! I think I'll go splash in some puddles now!"

The children repeat the phrase with their puppets. Put the terrier puppet away.

Teacher:	Make your dogs splash in puddles. Everybody say, "Splash, splash, splash."

Demonstrate the splash gesture using the puppet. Continue acting out the story in this manner until Small Brown Dog retrieves his collar. Ask the children to remember what Small Brown Dog likes to do, and act out each verb as the children mention them, ending as follows:

Teacher:	And my name is . . .
Children:	Patch!
Teacher:	Patch liked to do lots of things. But there were things he liked to do that were not in the book. My Patch likes to jump. Can we all jump? Jump! Jump! Jump! What other things does Patch like to do?

Follow-up

Having established that Patch has a poor memory, he may be used in subsequent lessons for review on a variety of topics. Patch may be present as a concept is introduced (the letter *P* in his name), yet still require the children to review the concept because he has forgotten it just a day later. ("Oh, no! Children, do you remember what letter Patch's name begins with?")

Mushroom in the Rain

FIG 6-6 Cast of characters for "Mushroom in the Rain" (bird, butterfly, mouse, red ant, rabbit, and fox). Instructions for puppets are on pages 177–182.

Basis for lesson

Mushroom in the Rain, adapted from the original Russian by Mirra Ginsburg; illustrated by Jose Aruego and Arianne Dewey.

Character type

Animals

Puppet use

Puppet show

Drama techniques

Providing language for a story, book with sequence (page 69)

Content

This lesson focuses on sequencing as the children remember the ordinal numbers of the characters' entrance. This lesson also gives children an opportunity to practice their oracy, an important part of emergent literacy.

Materials

One small plain umbrella (manual rather than automatic) to be operated by an adult only, ant puppet, butterfly puppet, mouse puppet, bird puppet, rabbit puppet, fox puppet, frog puppet. Optional: caterpillar puppet and ladybug puppet; multiples of some characters can be used, such as two mice or three birds.

Preparation

1) Develop a picture walk. The book does not have repetitive dialogue when each animal goes under the mushroom, so it must

be provided. For instance, "Help! I'm getting wet. Look, a mushroom. I'll hide under there."

2) Create a gesture for the children to use with the repetitive phrase.

3) Run through the lesson without the children present.

Note

This book includes a picture of hillsides that are white. Children may think this is snow and find the illustration confusing. The teacher may want to discuss this, or color the hills green.

Beginning the lesson

Seat the children so they can all see the book. Show the cover of the book and read the title. Establish a comprehensive understanding of mushrooms. Bring in a mushroom for the children to touch. Perhaps let them taste a mushroom. Show a picture of how large a mushroom can grow. Do a picture walk of *Mushroom in the Rain*. Discuss with the children the lie the animals tell to save the rabbit. Make sure that the children understand that it is not appropriate to lie in most circumstances.

Lesson with suggested dialogue

Open the umbrella slightly.

Teacher: I think this umbrella looks like a mushroom. Let's wiggle our fingers over our heads to pretend to be rain. We can make some rain noise, and watch our umbrella mushroom grow.

Give one child the red ant puppet and show him how to hold it.

Teacher: All right, class, we're ready to start our story. What is the weather like in the book? That's right, let's all make it rain.

The children pat their legs or do a rain gesture as practiced.

Teacher: What does the ant say as it starts to rain?

Let the child say as much as he can. A child with well-developed language skills may come out with an appropriate phrase or sentence on the first try. Others may just come up with a word or two, such as:

"Mushroom!" Praise the child for knowing the answer, then give the child a complete sentence to repeat. Others may need assistance with the language even to get started. Cue the students with the gesture that represents the repetitive phrase.

Teacher: **Can you have your ant say, "Help, I'm getting wet"?**

Let the child repeat the sentence.

Teacher: (*prompting child*) **Look, a mushroom!**

Let the child repeat the sentence.

Teacher: (*prompting child*) **I'll hide under there.**

Let the child repeat the sentence, then direct him to stand under the umbrella. If a classroom management technique is needed here, ask the child to leave his puppet under the umbrella and go back to his seat. Give another child the butterfly puppet and show her how to hold it. Ask the class to make it rain again.

Teacher: (*prompting child*) **Butterfly, what do you say, since it is raining so hard?**

Again, let the child respond to the best of her ability. Assist the child to ensure a successful language experience, regardless of the child's skill level.

Teacher: (*prompting child*) **The butterfly says, "Help, I'm getting wet. I'll hide under that mushroom."**

Let the child repeat the sentences. Direct the child with the butterfly puppet to ask the ant:

Teacher: (*prompting child*) **Can I hide under there?**

Let the child repeat the sentence. Encourage the ant to respond.

Teacher: (*prompting child*) **I don't know. There's not much room, but okay.**

Let the child repeat the sentence. Repeat the scene using a mouse puppet. Encourage both the ant and butterfly to respond together. Repeat the scene again in turn using the bird puppet, having the ant, butterfly, and mouse all respond to the bird. Use additional characters as needed, or use multiple mice, birds, and butterflies. Give one or more children a rabbit puppet and demonstrate how to work it. Ask the class to make it rain again.

Teacher: *(prompting child)* **What does the rabbit say?**

Let the child respond to the best of his ability, then feed him the lines to be repeated.

Teacher: *(prompting child)* **Help! Help! Help! The fox is after me. Hide me, please!**

Let the child repeat the sentence. Help the children hide the rabbit. Review with the children the fact that they do not want the fox to find the rabbit. Give a child the fox puppet. Demonstrate how to work it. Ask the class to make it rain again. Ask the child manipulating the fox to remember what was said in the book. If she has difficulty, feed her the lines.

Teacher: *(prompting child)* **Fox, say, "I'm hungry. Grrr, I smell a rabbit. Is there a rabbit here?"**

Teacher: *(prompting all animals)* **No, there's no rabbit here.**

Direct the fox to sniff around the mushroom.

Teacher: *(prompting fox puppet)* **I smell a rabbit.**

Teacher: *(prompting animals)* **There is no rabbit here. Go away.**

Teacher: *(prompting fox)* **Harumph.**

Ask the class to make sunshine, using gestures and saying, "Shine, shine."

Teacher: **What happened after the rain stopped? Can you make the ant say, "How did we all fit under the mushroom?"**

Let the child repeat the sentence. Give a child the frog puppet and demonstrate how to use it. Have the child put his frog puppet up on the mushroom. Assist the child in saying the following:

                Ribbit, ribbit. Don't you know a mushroom grows in the rain?

Wind

Basis of lesson

Gilberto and the Wind, by Marie Hall Ets

Character type

Inanimate object

Puppet use

Specialty puppet

Drama techniques

Introducing a puppet (page 66), object puppet (page 18)

Content

This activity supports emergent literacy (alphabetic principle, children's literature, vocabulary). It is an exercise in comparison and verbalizing anticipated events, and can be used in units on science or seasons.

Materials

Hair dryer or hand fan puppet, leaves with letters on them, electrical outlet

Preparation

1) This activity is part of a larger study of the wind. The children should have discussed the wind and its definition, experienced it on the playground and with science experiments. They should know that the wind can't be seen, but its effects can be seen. Read *Gilberto and the Wind.*

2) Select a hair dryer made since 1990 that does not contain asbestos for this project. Decorate the hair dryer with yarn over the nozzle to make a mustache, and cardboard eyes facing the same direction as the nozzle. A hat or cape on the handle is

FIG 6-7 Mr. Wind from "Wind"

optional. If the teacher is unable to use a hair dryer, a hand fan can be decorated in the same manner to be the wind puppet. [FIGURE 6-7]

3) Cut tree leaf shapes out of construction paper. Label both sides of each leaf with the letters *W, I, N,* or *D*. Multiples of four may be used for a large class.

4) Practice the lesson without the children present.

Beginning the lesson

Seat the children in a circle. Reserve a place in the circle for the puppeteer near the outlet used for the hair dryer puppet. Discuss "imagination" with the children and how they use it on a regular basis.

Lesson with suggested dialogue

Teacher: Do you remember when Gilberto and the wind were playing with leaves? Raise your hand if you can tell me what the wind did to the leaves.

The children respond by describing the pictures of the leaves blowing in the book.

Teacher: Can we see the wind in that picture? Raise your hand if you have an answer.

The children answer.

Teacher: If you could see the wind, what do you think it would look like? Raise your hand if you can tell me what it looks like in your imagination.

The children describe what they think the wind looks like. If they are unable to answer, the teacher moves on.

Teacher: Well, I made a puppet to show what the wind looks like in my imagination. I'd like to show it to you.

The teacher brings out the hair dryer puppet, plugged in at the wall with an extension cord if necessary.

Teacher: My idea of the wind is that he has a long nose, big eyes, and a mustache. Does the wind really look like that?

The children confirm that the wind cannot be seen.

Teacher: I want to show you how my puppet, Mr. Wind, talks. He talks by blowing.

Turn on hair dryer so the yarn mustache blows out at an angle.

Teacher: Look at Mr. Wind! When he talks, the wind from his mouth blows his mustache. Would you like to feel Mr. Wind blow on your face?

Go around to each child, and blow lightly on her face unless she refuses. If the child refuses, ask if you can blow on her hand. If not, move on to the next child until everyone has had an opportunity to feel the wind.

Teacher: Well, you could all feel Mr. Wind blow on your face. Do you think my Mr. Wind puppet could blow leaves like the ones with Gilberto in the book? What do you think would happen?

The children anticipate the activity, and describe what they think will happen.

Teacher: I'm going to try to find out what happens when Mr. Wind blows the leaves.

Get out the construction paper leaves, and lay them out to spell wind, *reading from left to right from the children's point of view.*

Teacher: Look at that! These leaves have some letters on them. Who can tell me what this letter is?

The teacher points to each letter in succession, letting the children name them all. If the children are able to sound out the word, they are invited to do so.

Teacher: When you put these letters together, they spell the word "wind." Well, are you ready to see if the leaves blow? Look for the leaf that blows the farthest and the leaf that blows the highest. Don't touch them until I say, so that we can look at where they land.

Turn on the hair dryer, and blow the leaves a few feet.

Teacher: Wow! Mr. Wind really did blow the leaves. Raise your hand if you can tell me the name of the letter on the leaf that blew the farthest.

A child answers.

Teacher: Who can tell me the name of the letter on the
                            leaf that blew the highest?

A child answers.

Teacher: Does anyone else have a different answer?

Allow the children to answer.

Teacher: Raise your hand if you can bring me the leaf
                            with the letter *W* on it.

Ask for the leaves one by one, in the order of the word wind. *The
teacher should choose children who did not make comparative observations about the leaves blowing. Go through the whole process
again. She may ask different questions when the leaves blow.*

Teacher: Who can raise their hand and tell me which
                            leaf landed closest to Gracie? Who can tell me
                            which leaf landed closest to me? Which leaf is
                            closest to you? Which leaf twirled the most in
                            the air? Which leaf was in the air for the
                            longest time?

*After each child has had a chance to answer a question about the
leaves or return one of the leaves to the teacher, the activity is ended.*

Teacher: Well, I'm putting the leaves away, and it's time
                            for Mr. Wind to say good-bye. Would you like
                            him to come around and say good-bye to each
                            of you?

*If the consensus is yes, the teacher quickly blows each child again
before packing away Mr. Wind.*

Puppet Lessons Based on Oral Traditions

Stories from the oral tradition are those that most children know, such as fairy tales, folktales, and myths. Using puppets to tell these stories offers students another version of a tale they are familiar with, promoting contrast and comparison. Discussion of the story and how it can be told with puppets increases language skills, including vocabulary, and gives students the opportunity to practice sequencing. Puppets also provide an interpretation of the story that encourages visual cues and assists in memory of the tale. This promotes emergent literacy skills, such as understanding concepts about the story. Most traditional stories can be told successfully using the puppet lesson techniques presented below. For example, the story of "Goldilocks and the Three Bears" can be told using finger puppets in the same way as "The Three Little Pigs" described in this chapter.

Because the children are familiar with traditional stories, a number of techniques are available to the teacher that might not be otherwise. The cloze technique works well with these stories. Teachers can also have the children help tell the story as it unfolds, using a question-and-answer format. In this scenario, the teacher may say, "What did Goldilocks do next?" after telling how Goldilocks entered the bears' home. At this point, one of three things may happen. A student may volunteer a viable answer, such as "She sat in the baby bear's chair," or "She tried the bear's porridge." Alternatively, a child may suggest something that is unrelated to the story being told, such as "Goldilocks turned on the music and started to dance." In the interest of including all of the children's ideas, these answers may be incorporated into the story with a little ingenuity on the teacher's part. She may say, "That's right! She turned on Elvis Presley singing 'Just Want to Be Your Teddy Bear,' and started to do the twist. What happened after that?" The third possibility is that a child might offer an answer that is out of chronological order. An example of this would be if the teacher asks, "What did Goldilocks do when she went into the bears' house?" and a child responded, "She went upstairs and laid in their beds!" In this case, the teacher should accept the answer, "Yes! She did go upstairs, but first she did something else. Does anyone know what it was?" Then when it is time for Goldilocks to try out the bears' beds, the teacher may refer back to the child who mentioned it first, saying, "Lavonda knows what happened next. Lavonda, what did Goldilocks do when she went upstairs?" The success of letting the children tell the story through a question-and-answer format lies in the teacher's willingness to include all answers, and make up new parts of the story if the children offer them.

Knowledge of the story can also make it possible for the children to make their own puppets and scenery from their mind's eye, rather than following specific pictures in a book. This kind of involvement gives the children an ownership of the project, and makes it less teacher centered.

Jack and the Beanstalk

Basis for lesson

Oral tradition

Character types

People, animal, fantasy

Puppet use

Puppet actor

Drama techniques

Cloze technique (page 22), using the bare hand as a puppet (page 14), using voice to portray emotion (page 44), children telling the story through questions and answers (page 27).

Content

This lesson gives children practice with their fine motor skills in particular because it uses the bare hand. It also gives the children a choral speaking experience. It can be used during a study of fairy tales.

Materials

None

Preparation

Practice the lesson without the children present. Familiarize the students with the story of Jack and the beanstalk. Discuss the different versions the students are familiar with to establish their validity. Assure students that if they know another version, it is not "wrong."

Lesson with suggested dialogue

Teacher: Do you remember the story of Jack and the beanstalk? Who is in the story?

Let the students respond until they have mentioned Jack, his mother, and the Giant.

Teacher: Let's make Jack look like this.

Hold up a hand using the fingers and thumb as a mouth.

Teacher: As you know, Jack was a very lazy boy. He didn't want to do anything. He didn't want to . . .

Fill in familiar tasks done around the classroom, such as clear his lunch tray, feed the fish, wash his hands.

FIG 6-8 through FIG 6-12 Rodrigo Pincheira demonstrates the hand/arm positions for "Jack and the Beanstalk," (6-8 Jack with his mom, 6-9 the Cow, 6-10 the Funny Little Man, 6-11 the Giant, 6-12 the Chicken)

Teacher:	He didn't even like to talk. All he ever said was "Fiddle-dee-dee." *(said with a sigh to indicate disinterest)*. Can you say fiddle-dee-dee with me and move your hand like this?

Have the children repeat the phrase, imitating the sullen tone, and encourage them to use the hand gestures throughout.

Teacher:	Sometimes Jack was really mad, and then he would say, "Fiddle-dee-dee!"

Have the children repeat the phrase quickly with an angry tone this time.

Teacher:	Sometimes Jack was really scared, and then he would say, "Fiddle-dee-dee!"

Have the children repeat the phrase slowly with a quivering voice this time.

Teacher:	Sometimes Jack would see something that was amazing, and then he would say, "Fiddle-deeeeeee-deeeeeee!"

The phrase is said stretching out the vowels, loudly with the tone ascending then descending during the last syllable. Have the children repeat it in that manner.

Teacher:	Now, Jack lived with his mother, who looked like this.

Hold up your other hand identical to your Jack hand.

Teacher:	See how much Jack looks like his mother? Jack's mother didn't know what to do with Jack, so mostly what she said was "Oh, Jack." *(said in a long-suffering tone, with a sigh and a weary droop in tone at the end)*
	Now we need some other characters in our story. First there is a cow. And she looks like this.

Make a fist and extend the pinkie finger and either the forefinger or the thumb to represent two horns. Let the children make their own "cows."

Teacher:	Everybody make your cow say, "Mooooooo." Good. Next we need a funny little man. He looks like this.

Make a fist. Curl your thumb around the nails of the other four fingers. Raise your fingers to make the upper lip talk.

Teacher: He says, "Hey, I'm a funny little man!" Can you make your little men say that with me?

Let the children repeat the phrase, using their hands as little men.

Teacher: Now of course we need a giant. He looks like this.

Hold your hand as you did Jack, but high over your head.

Teacher: I'm sure you've heard the giant saying lots of things, but my giant says, "Fee, fie, foe, fum. I smell someone chewing bubble gum!" Everyone say that with me in your big giant voice.

The children repeat the phrase with loud voices.

Teacher: We may need some other characters, but we'll figure those out when we come to them. Okay, how do all good fairy tales start?

Let the children respond until someone mentions, "Once upon a time."

Teacher: Once upon a time! That's a wonderful way to start. Okay, let's say that together. Once upon a time, there lived a little boy named Jack. All he ever said was . . .

Hold up one hand to demonstrate and speak along with the class. The children answer, "Fiddle-dee-dee."

Teacher: He lived with his mother who said . . .

Hold up a second hand to speak to the Jack hand. Children answer, "Oh, Jack."

Teacher: One day Jack's mom said, "Take the cow and sell her." Have the mother say that to Jack.

Children imitate the teacher.

Teacher as Jack's mom: And buy some food.

Have the mother hand speak the phrase, and pause to see if the children understand the convention and have their own mother hands repeat the phrase.

Teacher:	Jack didn't want to do this, so he said, "Fiddle-dee-dee."

Children imitate the teacher.

Teacher:	So Jack and the cow . . . Moooo. Everybody say, "Mooooo."

Children imitate the teacher.

Teacher:	. . . set off for town. They didn't get very far when up jumped the funny little man.

Make the cow hand into the funny little man.

Teacher as funny little man: Hey, I'm a funny little man!

Children imitate the teacher. Continue to use the funny little man hand.

Teacher as funny little man: Hey, Jack. I'll buy your cow.

Children imitate the teacher.

Teacher as funny little man: I'll give you three magic beans.

Children imitate the teacher.

Teacher:	Jack was excited because he didn't want to walk all the way to town. He said, "Fiddle-dee-dee," and walked home.

Children imitate the teacher.

Teacher:	When Jack's mom saw the three beans, she said, "Oh, Jack."

Have the mother hand look into the open palm of the other hand. Children imitate the teacher.

Teacher:	She took the beans and threw them out the window.

Have the mother hand pick up the beans from the palm of the other hand and one by one throw them over your shoulder. Children imitate the teacher.

Teacher:	And they went to sleep hungry. (snoring noise)

Hold both hands in the Jack and mother positions. Put the hands parallel to the floor to sleep, then synchronize the mouths with the snoring sound. Children imitate the teacher.

Teacher:	While they were sleeping, the beanstalk began to grow.

One hand twines its way upward to be the beanstalk.

Teacher:	It grew and grew and grew and grew. The next morning, Jack woke up.

Use the nonbeanstalk hand to be Jack, and move the wrist up and down to look at the beanstalk.

Teacher:	Jack looked at the beanstalk and was so excited that he said, "Fiddle-deeeee-deeee!"

Children imitate the teacher.

Teacher:	Jack began to climb the beanstalk.

Move the Jack hand up along the vine hand. Children imitate the teacher.

Teacher:	He climbed, and he climbed, and he climbed, and he climbed. When he got to the top, he looked around.

Rotate the wrist to make Jack's head look around. Children imitate the teacher.

Teacher:	Someone has to tell me what he saw.

Children respond. Whatever the children volunteer is used next in the story. If the giant is mentioned, the teacher says:

Teacher:	You're right! But the giant was asleep.

Make the giant sleep by extending your arm full length, parallel to the floor, and lip-sync a loud snore. If the children say that Jack saw a castle first, respond:

Teacher:	You're right! He was so excited that he said fiddle-dee-dee and crawled under the giant door.

Children may mention the giant's wife, a cook, a table, a golden harp, and so forth. Whatever is offered is incorporated into the story. Eventually, the story will end up with Jack finding the goose (or chicken) that lays the golden eggs. However, the interim parts of the story may be improvised as dictated by the children's suggestions.

Teacher:	That's right! Ross said that Jack saw a chicken laying eggs. Have you ever seen a chicken lay a golden egg? Well, this is how it looks. Buck . . .

buck, buck, buck . . . Buck . . . buck, buck, buck . . . Buck . . . buck, buck, buck . . . Buuuuuuck.

*If the child does not say "**Goose**" as in Grimm's fairy tale, use whatever bird is suggested. To make the bird, hold out a fist, then touch the thumb and forefinger together to make a beak. Synchronize the beak with the buck sound. The bucks get louder and louder until the last buuuuuck is said with a sigh to indicate that the egg has been laid. Children imitate teacher.*

Teacher: Jack couldn't believe his eyes, he said,

Let the children fill in "Fiddle-dee-dee!"

Teacher: . . . and he picked up the chicken and ran down the beanstalk.

Have one hand grab at an imaginary chicken, then move it down the beanstalk. Children imitate teacher.

Teacher: All of that squawking woke up the giant. He said . . .

Let the children say, "Fee, fie, foe, fum. I smell someone chewing bubble gum."

Teacher: Jack spat out his bubble gum, "Pitooey!" onto a leaf and climbed down the beanstalk even faster.

Children imitate teacher.

Teacher: And the giant came after him!

Hold one hand up in the air and sway it back and forth as if the giant is stomping while running. Children imitate teacher.

Teacher: Jack was going just as fast as he possibly could.

Move the Jack hand down the beanstalk arm quickly. Children imitate teacher.

Teacher: And the giant came after him!

Hold one hand up in the air and sway it back and forth as if the giant is stomping while running. Children imitate teacher.

Teacher: Jack was going so fast, he couldn't even see what he was doing!

Move the Jack hand down the beanstalk arm quickly. Children imitate teacher.

Teacher: **Then the giant stepped on the bubble gum and that slowed him down.**

Pretend one foot is stuck to the floor. Children imitate teacher.

Teacher: **Jack got to the bottom of the beanstalk, picked up an ax, and chopped and chopped and chopped.**

The teacher uses his whole body to mime picking up the ax and chopping the beanstalk. Children imitate teacher.

Teacher: **The beanstalk with the giant on it went, "Neeeeeahhhhhh, Splat!"**

Have the beanstalk arm drop suddenly. Children imitate teacher.

Teacher: **The giant made a big hole in the ground, it filled up with water, and that's how we got the Chesapeake Bay.**

Teachers may want to substitute a nearby familiar body of water.

Teacher: **When Jack's mom saw the golden egg, she said, "Oh, Jack!"**

"Oh, Jack," is said loudly with an approving tone of voice. Children imitate teacher.

Teacher: **And Jack said, "I love you, Mom!" and gave her a big kiss.**

Teacher uses the Jack hand and the children imitate teacher.

Teacher: **And they all lived . . .**

The children fill in,   **"Happily ever after!"**

The Three Little Pigs

Basis for lesson

Oral tradition

Character types

Animals

Use of puppet

Puppet actors

Drama techniques used

Cloze technique (page 22), using finger puppets (page 12), using props (page 51)

FIG 6-13 Straw house, stick house, and brick house with the Three Little Pigs and the Big Bad Wolf (finger puppets)

Content

"The Three Little Pigs" gives children an opportunity for creative problem solving, discussing emotions such as the fear the pigs have of the wolf, and how those emotions might be handled. It is appropriate for curriculum units on fairy tales and emotions.

Materials

A handful of straw, a handful of sticks, a brick, three pig finger puppets, one wolf finger puppet, two file folders decorated like a straw house and stick house, respectively, two file folders making a brick house as described below (or alternatively, classroom building blocks shaped and decorated like bricks).

Preparation

1) Try on the finger puppets and practice with them. Adjust the puppets to fit the appropriate fingers. For ease in manipulation, do not put puppets on consecutive fingers. Put a pig puppet on the pinkie, one on the forefinger, and one on the thumb. Put the wolf puppet on the forefinger of the hand in opposition to that of the pigs. Make sure the wolf puppet slips on and off easily, and that the pig puppets are secure.

2) To make the pigs' houses, use four file folders. Decorate a folder on the outside with straw and another with sticks. Set them up on end to make two walls of a house. Glue two folders together to make a three-sided house with no floor or ceiling. Decorate the outside with bricks, and decorate the inside with a fireplace. Alternatively, for the brick house, you may use classroom building blocks and let the finger puppet build her brick house on a tabletop during the story.

3) Practice the lesson without the children present.

Beginning the lesson

Familiarize students with "The Three Little Pigs." Let the children see the finger puppets up close and touch them. Let the children touch the straw, sticks, and brick. The teacher may discuss different versions the students are familiar with to establish the validity of each version. Assure students that if they know another version, it is not "wrong."

Lesson with suggested dialogue

Put the three pig puppets on one hand.

Teacher: I have a story that you can help me tell. How do fairy tales begin?

Let children respond until someone mentions, "Once upon a time."

Teacher: Oh, that's a good way to start. Let's all say that together: Once upon a time, there were three little pigs. The first little pig was a cutie named Curly because of his curly tail. He was very friendly, and loved to talk to people. In fact, he wants to talk to you right now.

Hold up one finger with the first pig puppet on it. The other puppets will be in view, but they will be bent down, facing your hand. Choose a distinctive voice that is comfortable to use.

Teacher as Curly: Hi! I'm Curly. Oh, you look like such interesting boys and girls!

Have the puppet turn to speak to your face.

Teacher as Curly: I'd like to meet them. Is that okay?

Teacher: I think that would be nice. Why don't you just walk around the circle to talk to them?

Teacher as Curly: I think I would like to meet them, but I might be too tired. Does anyone here get tired? *(to first child)* Lani, do you ever feel lazy and tired?

Move around the circle letting the children see the small finger puppet up close one at a time. The children may say as much as they want about feeling tired or lazy as time permits.

Teacher: Guess what? Curly has a brother named Larry. Can you say hello to Larry?

Hold up a second pig, and use a voice distinct from the first pig.

Teacher as Larry: Howdy, pardners! How ya doin' there? Hooboy, this is a mighty fine lookin' bunch of kiddies. Hey, what's yer name? Ya know what I was just sittin' here thinkin' about? I was thinkin' about buildin' a house. What can you tell me about your house? What color is your house?

(to second child) **Oh, do you live in an apartment, Mei Li?**

Have the second pig go around, talking about homes as long as time permits. Children who do not want to chat with the pig should not be forced to, but should still be fully included in the exercise.

Teacher:	Well, you know, the pig family is even bigger than that! They have a sister whose name is Maureen. Everyone calls her Mo though. Can you say "hello" to Mo?

Hold up the third pig, and have her speak using a distinctive third voice.

Teacher as Mo:	Oh, I'm so glad to see you children! I've been thinking about something that is bothering me a little. I've realized that I am just the tiniest bit afraid of wolves. Not screaming, nightmare afraid, just sort of uncomfortable. I think I am the only one who is a little afraid of something. Do you know anyone else who has this problem? Do you think I am the only one who gets a teensy-weensy bit scared of something?

Let the third pig go around the circle, discussing fears with each child as time allows.

Teacher as Mo:	Oh, you've made me feel so much better! I know that I'm not the only one who sometimes feels a little afraid. You all said such comforting things.
Teacher:	Well, the three little pigs lived in one little house, and it began to get crowded. Finally, the little pigs went out into the world to build their own houses. The first little pig didn't like to work very hard. He felt tired and lazy, so he built his house out of straw.

With the hand that does not have puppets on it, set up the file folder decorated with straw. Let the first pig puppet move around the folder house to show it is being built.

Teacher:	The second pig was very interested in houses, but he didn't want to spend too much time, so he built his house out of sticks.

With the hand that does not have puppets on it, set up the file folder decorated with sticks. Let the second pig puppet move around the folder house to show it is being built.

Teacher as Mo: My mommy and daddy always told me that if I was afraid of something, I should not stay quiet. I should talk to a grown-up about what was making me scared, and make a plan about what to do. Well, I talked to you and your teacher about my fear of wolves. Now I'm going to make a plan. I'm going to make a house of bricks. It might take a long time, but I'm going to make a house of bricks that will keep me safe from wolves.

With the hand that does not have puppets on it, set up the box house decorated with bricks. Let the third pig puppet move around the box house to show it is being built.

Teacher: Well, just as soon as the pigs were done building their houses, along came a wolf.

Put the wolf puppet on the empty hand. Use a distinct fourth voice for the wolf.

Teacher as Wolf: Tra-la-la-la-la. Oh! I am so hungry. *(Wolf to the teacher)* You know, these children look like they might be hungry too. Are any of you ever hungry?

As time permits, have the wolf discuss hunger and what the children like to eat.

Teacher as Wolf: Here is a new house I've never seen before. Sniff, sniff. It smells like there is a piggy in there. Hummmmm. Do you know what wolves like to eat? That's right! Little piggies. And this house is only made of straw. It looks like it could just blow away!

Move the wolf puppet close to the house.

Teacher as Wolf: Little pig, little pig, let me in!

Hold up the first pig puppet on the other side of the folder.

Teacher as Curly: Not by the hair of my . . .

Let children respond: Chinny, chin, chin!

Move the wolf as if speaking on the other side of the folder.

Teacher as Wolf: Then I'll huff, and I'll puff, and I'll . . .

Let children respond: Blow your house in.

Teacher: *(while the wolf puppet blows on the house)* Can you blow right from where you're sitting and help the wolf? Oh, no! The straw house fell over! Where should the little pig go? What should he do?

Let the children respond until someone answers:

He should go to the second little pig's house.

Have the first little pig run over to the stick house folder. Repeat the above scenario, holding up the two pigs to speak the pig(s)' lines. Repeat the scenario a third time until the line:

Teacher: Can you blow and help the wolf? Uh-oh. The house isn't blowing over. It looks like Mo's plan worked.

Teacher as Wolf: Oh, goodness. Now I'm really tired from all that blowing, but I'm still hungry, because I didn't get to eat any little pigs.

Teacher: Poor, poor wolf. He is so hungry and tired. But the little pigs don't want to be eaten up either. This is a real problem. Both the wolf and the pigs are our friends. How do you think we can solve the problem? What do you think the wolf or the pigs could do to make things better?

Let the children respond with their ideas, taking as many suggestions as possible. Choose one or two to act out with the finger puppets.

Lesson Techniques with Puppets

Lesson techniques differ from other types of activities in that they can be paired with a wide variety of stories or can be used as part of a curriculum unit when there is no plot involved. These techniques do not necessarily have a beginning, middle, or end, but can be thought of as a method used in a larger context. For instance, Sam the Dog may be used to review a lesson, field trip, or experience the children have had. It can be the closing of a larger lesson on nutrition, such as that described below, and be the only part of the lesson or unit that uses a puppet.

FIG 6-14 Michele Valeri holds Julius, who is a glove/rod puppet with two hand rods. Julius can express many emotions with posture and arm positions. Here he is waving shyly.

Julius: Silent Puppet/Lesson Review

Developed by Michele Valeri

Basis for lesson

Lesson technique

Character type

Animal

Puppet use

Teacher-manipulated task assistant, reward puppet

Drama techniques

Silent puppet (page 45), classroom management through puppets (page 31)

Content

This puppet technique can be used for review to stimulate emergent literacy and to assess story comprehension.

Materials

Puppet, book

Preparation

Practice the lesson without the children present.

Beginning the lesson

Seat the children in a circle or as desired. Put on the Julius puppet.

Lesson with suggested dialogue

Teacher:	This is my friend Julius.

Julius looks at every child for a second and then whispers in the teacher's ear.

Teacher:	Julius says hello.

Julius waves at the class and waits for the children to wave back or say hello. Then Julius whispers in the teacher's ear again.

Teacher:	Julius wants me to tell you that he doesn't talk out loud. He only talks to me and even then he only whispers in my ear.

Julius nods in agreement and then whispers in the teacher's ear again.

Teacher:	Yes, Julius. I'll tell them. Julius wants to show you what he does best. You see, Julius is a great listener. This is Julius listening.

Hold the puppet with his chin elevated so he looks like he is listening.

Teacher:	Julius, what did you hear?

Julius whispers in the puppeteer's ear.

Teacher:	Julius says he heard you giggling.

Julius nods in agreement again and whispers again.

Teacher:	Julius wants to know if you are good listeners. Are you good listeners? Would you like to listen with Julius?

Julius looks at the children nodding yes.

Teacher:	Okay, everybody. Let's listen with Julius. Close your eyes and just listen.

Encourage everyone to listen with Julius by modeling the behavior.

Teacher:	Jevan, what did you hear?

Students answer, reporting sounds they heard in the school, such as talking in the hall. Julius nods in agreement.

Teacher:	Julius, you heard that too? Did anyone hear anything different? Shaneequa, what did you hear?

The children answer, and Julius nods and whispers.

Teacher: Julius says that you are good listeners.

Julius nods and whispers.

Teacher: Julius wants me to show you the book I brought today. Julius, can you point to the words for me?

The puppeteer holds up the book and reads the title. Julius points with his nose to each word as she pronounces it.

Teacher: This says, "Big Al." It's one of Julius's favorites.

Julius nods yes vigorously.

Alternatively, the teacher may hold the book upside down. Julius tips upside down to read the words, then whispers in the teacher's ear. "Oh, it's upside down."

The teacher puts the book down and picks it up sideways. Julius shakes his head no.

Teacher: Oops. The book is sideways.

The teacher finally holds it correctly and reads the title.

Teacher: Now Julius is going to do what he does best, which is to listen. He loves to listen to books. So he's going to sit over here and listen.

The teacher takes Julius off her hand and props Julius up on a shelf or a desk. The puppet may be used for review once circle time is over.

Teacher: Julius, what did you think about the story?

Julius whispers in the teacher's ear.

Teacher: Julius thought the little fish were funny.

Julius opens his mouth and mimes laughing, then he whispers again.

Teacher: Julius liked when Big Al tried to make friends. Yes, I liked that too.

Julius whispers again.

Teacher: Julius wants to know why the little fish swam away from Big Al. Who can tell Julius why the little fish swam away?

The discussion about the book and the story dramatization shouldn't go on for more than a few minutes before Julius whispers again and yawns.

Teacher: Julius says it's time for his nap, so say good night to Julius. Wave good-bye, Julius.

Julius waves good-bye before being put back in his sack.

Book Puppet: Introducing Children's Literature

FIG 6-15 A talking book puppet

Basis for lesson

Lesson technique

Character type

Inanimate object

Puppet use

Teacher-manipulated task assistant, specialty puppet, reward puppet

Drama techniques

Lesson technique (page 120), object puppet (page 18)

Content

The book puppet assists in exposing children to literature and in their understanding of it. This is done through story-version compare-and-contrast activities, word cards that support concepts about print, and discussion of the books supporting concepts about story. This lesson technique also provides an experience in sorting and classification.

Materials

A hardcover book with no pictures on the cover, tagboard eyes, optional tagboard tongue, or other facial features

Preparation

1) Select an appropriate book. Create eyes for the book by cutting out ovals or circles from white tagboard. Attach the circles to the front cover of the book, imagining that the spine is the top of the head and the front cover opening and closing is a mouth. Draw black dots to indicate pupils on the eyes, being careful to make it look as if the eyes are able to focus on an

audience—the class. A nose, freckles, or other facial features are optional. A tongue may be placed inside the front cover.

2)   Practice opening and closing the front cover of the book while lip-syncing in front of a mirror to make sure it seems as though the book is talking.

3)   Practice the lesson without the children present.

Beginning the lesson

Seat the children in a circle or as desired. Pull out the book puppet.

Lesson with suggested dialogue

Teacher:	I have a friend who came to talk to us today. He may look familiar to you—you may know this puppet.

Pull out the book puppet. Children usually respond, "It's a book!"

Teacher:	That's right! It's a book. It has pages, and a spine, and a cover. But wait. What's on the cover?

Let the children respond until one says, "Eyes."

Teacher:	Right! This book has eyes, so I like to pretend it can talk. Books are full of great stories, so let's see if this one can tell a story.

The teacher may then have the puppet book tell a story. A short, familiar story is recommended as the puppet is limited in its capabilities and is more successfully used for introductions.

Further lesson techniques for use with this book

STORY INTRODUCTION

Use the above dialogue to introduce stories told orally. For younger children, loose-leaf pictures may be inserted between the pages of the book and held up at the appropriate time in the story to illustrate it. Alternatively, teachers working on concepts about print may insert word cards representing key words from the story between the pages.

STORY INITIATION PICTURES

Children may initiate original or oral tradition stories told by the teacher. The children each draw a picture, then "feed" it into the book. The book responds:

Teacher as Book: **Mmmm! So delicious. That picture tastes like the story of . . .**

The teacher can then tell a story triggered by the picture ("Goldilocks and the Three Bears" for a picture of a bear) or make up her own story if she is confident about her improvisation skills.

Alternatively, the pictures can be used as a sorting and classification exercise. To do this, the teacher selects at least two fairy tales and prepares pictures to represent each character in the stories. The class collectively selects the characters needed for a given story, then feeds them into the book in order to hear the book tell the story. The book comments in an enthusiastic manner, saying things like, "I'm hungry for a story! Please feed me!" or "Mmmmm! That is my favorite story taste!"

STORY REVIEW

To help the children review a familiar story, the book takes on a forgetful personality.

Teacher as Book: **I used to know a story, and it started once upon a time. It had bowls of porridge in it. Do you know what story I'm talking about? Can you help me remember what happens first in that story?**

COMPARE AND CONTRAST STORY VARIATIONS

Six-, seven-, and eight-year-olds enjoy comparing various versions of well-known stories such as "Little Red Riding Hood." To facilitate this interest and support concepts about the story, the book puppet can comment on these variations:

Teacher as Book: **And then the wolf ate the grandmother. Wait a minute! I don't want him to eat the sweet old grandmother! She made such good cookies. What else could happen instead?**

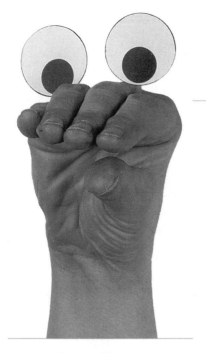

FIG 6-16 The Anything Puppet. Instructions for the puppet are on pages 183–184.

Anything Puppet

Basis for lesson

Lesson technique

Character type

Any character, as needed

Puppet use

Any use, as needed

Drama techniques

Exposed puppet (page 48), the bare hand as puppet (page 14), using the puppet's mouth for other than speaking (page 41)

Content

Anything Puppets exercise fine motor skills and support the children's imagination. It can be used in all curriculum units, as any kind of puppet character, and for most puppet uses.

Materials

Pipe cleaner, circles of tagboard, hot glue, felt-tip marker

Note

A similar puppet, Peepers, designed by the talented puppeteer Hobie Ford, is available commercially. It may be bought in lieu of making an Anything Puppet. The Anything Puppet is copyrighted by Ingrid Crepeau, preventing anyone from making and selling them. However, teachers are enthusiastically invited to make Anything Puppets for their own use in the classroom.

Preparation

1) Make the Anything Puppet as described in chapter 7.

2) Practice the lesson without the children present.

Lesson with suggested dialogue

Teacher:	I have a friend in my pocket. It's a very small, tiny, little puppet. It's so small, it fits in my pocket.

Put a hand in the pocket, move the hand in the pocket, and make a hiccuping sound.

Teacher:	Oh, dear! My puppet has the hiccups! Let's get it out here so we can see what's going on.

Pull out the Anything Puppet, put it on your hand, and have your hand (the puppet) hiccup.

Teacher:	Oh, dear! I have the hick- *(hiccup)* ups. What shall I do?

Let the children offer suggestions for ridding the puppet of hiccups. Act out the suggestions.

Teacher:	Oh, thank you! You got rid of my hiccups! I am the Anything Puppet, because I can be anything. Want to see me be tall?

Hold the hand overhead.

Teacher:	Look! I'm tall! I'm a giant! You look like ants down there. Oh, I'm getting dizzy. I'm coming down. Now do you want to see me be short?

Ask all the children to stand while the puppet is rested on the floor.

Teacher:	Oh, look! I'm short and you're tall. You look like giants! You're scaring me. Everybody sit down. I can be something else too. How 'bout if I am a dog? Woof! Woof! Woof! Slurp!

Lip-sync the barking, then use the thumb as a tongue and lick your own cheek. Make a horrible expression.

Teacher:	Ewwww! The dog kissed me.
Anything Puppet:	Would anyone else like a kiss?

Go around to each child and have the puppet kiss them if they indicate they would like it.

Teacher:	What else could the Anything Puppet be?

Let children respond with suggestions, and act them out as they are offered.

Follow-up

After this introduction, Anything Puppets may be handed out to the children. This must be done by placing the puppets one by one on each child's hand (as illustrated in chapter 7) so the child can manipulate it properly. Proper protocol for introducing puppets, including the puppet pledge, must be used. You can then guide the puppets in becoming a variety of animals. The Anything Puppets can be made available for free choice time. They are also useful to fill in for any missing characters in a puppet presentation. An excellent book to use with Anything Puppets is *Jump, Frog, Jump,* by Robert Kalan, as it gives the Anything Puppet an opportunity to portray several pond-dwelling animals. Alternatively, every child may have an Anything Puppet to be frogs, while the teacher portrays the other pond animals. Other ideas include adding hats, scarves, or other small costume pieces to create characters. Anything Puppets may be left inside of a book to act out the story.

Original Stories: Activities for Special Purposes

Perhaps the most creative and flexible way to use puppets is in making original stories and activities. This is an excellent learning experience for the children, supporting a myriad of emergent literacy skills. It also provides teachers with a way to originate a puppet activity for any occasion. There are several plots and lesson plans that can be used to create new stories. Several useful original story concepts have been described below, but these are not the only ones possible. Other original story ideas include, "Mommy must not love me because she forgot to kiss me," "Mommy must not love me because she's having another baby," "A child in a new situation," "Preparing for a journey," "Going on a trip," or "Someone's hurt—what can we do to help him?" These plots can be used over and over, and each time they will become a new story when different characters and plot details are "plugged in" to the story outline given. When using these universal plots, you should keep in mind that the story outlines can be combined or overlapped. For example, the "Going on a trip" and "A new situation" concepts can easily be combined to create a story about a child who is visiting Grandma for the summer, what the trip is like, and how daily life at Grandma's is different when she gets there. This story line could end up as several lesson plans touching on a wide range of key experiences or curricular goals that would be carried out over several days or even weeks.

Another reason to create an original story is to accommodate the puppets at hand. Any puppet can become a character in a story, and animals can easily be substituted for people in this situation. To take advantage of this flexibility, alternatives are listed for each lesson plan in this section. As always, creative teachers will not limit themselves to either the lesson plan or the suggested alterations listed.

Baby Learns a New Word

FIG 6-17 Baby Jimmy in a happy mood (simple rod puppet). Instructions for the puppet are on pages 185–187.

Basis for lesson

Original activity

Character type

People (baby)

Puppet use

Puppet as a student

Drama techniques

Puppet as student (page 21)

Content

An activity with a baby puppet can be created for units on family and cooperation, and can be used to learn or reinforce vocabulary. The baby puppet can also be used to review any material presented by the teacher.

Materials

Baby puppet

Preparation

1) Select a baby puppet. Any puppet may become a baby puppet by putting a bonnet or pacifier on it.

2) Practice the lesson without the children present.

Lesson with suggested dialogue

Teacher: **Who has a baby at home? Who can tell me about babies?**

Responses to expect include "Babies cry"; "Babies don't talk"; "Babies poop in diapers"; "Babies are funny"; "Babies are boring"; "Babies sleep all the time and you have to be really quiet"; or "Babies are stupid." The teacher should rephrase negative comments without dismissing what the child has offered. For example, "Babies are stupid" can be reinterpreted as "Babies are brand new and haven't learned anything yet."

Introduce the baby puppet. Bring out the puppet and hold it as you would hold a baby. Introduce it to the class with a name. Have it make funny baby sounds to engage the children. Have the puppet act out as many of the observations that the children made about babies as possible.

Teacher as Baby:	Waaaaah.
Teacher:	Don't cry, Emma. There, there now.
Teacher as Baby:	Bababa. *(raspberry noise)*
Teacher:	*(to baby)* You can't talk yet, Emma, but you are funny and cute. *(to children)* Everybody pick up their own pretend baby and hold it gently like this. Now rock the baby. I'll tell you a story about my nephew and the day his baby brother learned his first word. My nephew's name is Richard, and his baby brother is named Jimmy. Set your baby down in the pretend baby crib behind you, and we can act out the story.

Teacher sets down her puppet as well.

Teacher:	Every day Richard would come home from school and slam the door. Everyone, slam the door, *boom!*

Use a gesture with each action to assist the children in remembering the sequence. Use a hand movement that suggests a door closing on the word boom.

Teacher:	He would throw his backpack across the room. Everyone throw your imaginary backpack across the room: whisshh boom! Then he would stomp up the stairs. Everyone go stomp, stomp, stomp with your feet. Then he would

hear, "Waaaah!" His mom would rush up to him with the crying baby in her arms (*mime holding a baby*) and say, "Be a little more quiet, please. You woke up your baby brother." Everyone say that after me. "Be a little more quiet, please."

Class repeats the sentence.

Teacher as Mom: You woke up your baby brother.

Class repeats the sentence.

Teacher: Then Richard would say in a very loud voice, "Babies are boring!" Everyone say that.

Class repeats the sentence.

This entire first sequence in the story should be repeated as many as four times for younger children.

Teacher: Richard said, "I wish I was Tyrannosaurus rex, king of the dinosaurs!" Everyone say that.

Class repeats the sentence.

Teacher as Richard: "Then no one could tell me to be quiet." Everyone say that.

Class repeats the sentence.

Teacher: His mother would say, "Richard, go to your room and play quietly."

Teacher: Day after day it was the same thing. Richard would come home and do what? Boom! Whisshh boom! Stomp, stomp, stomp! Then he'd hear, "Waaaaaah!"

This time, the teacher should pick up the puppet.

Teacher: His mom would say, "Be a little more quiet, please. You woke up your baby brother." Everyone say, "Be a little more quiet, please."

Class repeats the sentence.

Teacher as Mom: "You woke up your baby brother."

Class repeats the sentence.

Teacher:	And Richard would say what?

The story cannot continue without the word dinosaur. *Children often forget "Babies are boring," but they usually remember "I wish I was a Tyrannosaurus rex, the king of the dinosaurs, then no one could tell me to be quiet!" without prompting. (If necessary, they may need to be prompted to say the word* dinosaur. *If they forget everything else that Richard said but the word* dinosaur, *it's fine.)*

Teacher:	Just then baby Jimmy said the word, "'saur!" And Richard's mom said, "Richard, you taught Jimmy his first word." Richard said, "I did? I did!" After that day, Richard came home from school and carefully closed the door: click. Everybody close the door carefully.

The children say "click" and perform the appropriate gesture.

Teacher:	He carefully put his backpack down in the corner. Phlumph. Everybody put down your backpack carefully.

The children say "phlumph" and perform the appropriate gesture.

Teacher:	He carefully tiptoed up the stairs. Tip toe, tip toe. *(Said with appropriate gesture.)* And he asked his mom, "May I try to teach Jimmy a new word when he wakes up?" Richard and Jimmy are all grown-up now. They like each other a lot. And they both agree their favorite word is dinosaur! What word should we try to teach my puppet baby today?

Pick one or two words suggested by the class. The baby should be a little silly to hold the children's attention. The baby should make three wrong and silly attempts to say the word before succeeding.

Teacher:	Baby, say "Hat."
Teacher as Baby:	Hot! Hot! Hot!
Teacher:	Class, help me out. Say "Hat" to the baby.

The class says the word.

Teacher as Baby:	Who! Who! Who!
Teacher:	Class, let's try again. Hat.

The class says the word.

Teacher as Baby:	Hut! Hut! Hut!
Teacher:	That's almost right. One more time. Class, say "Hat."

The class says the word.

Teacher as Baby:	Hat! Hat! Hat! Hat! Hat! Hat!
Teacher:	Very good, Baby Emma! That's enough.

Suggested alternatives

* Once the baby is introduced to the class, the students can teach the baby throughout the year. For example, the children can review colors, shapes, letters, and so on by teaching the baby all about them.

* The story may be changed to suit the needs of the teacher and the class. For example, if there is a problem with hitting in the classroom, the Richard character could become twins who fight loudly and wake the baby. The story could end with the twins working together to decide what word to teach the baby.

Surprise Party

Basis for lesson

Original activity

Character types

Animals

Puppet use

Puppet actors

Drama techniques

Using rod puppets (page 15), using puppet actors (page 23), using animal characters (page 25)

FIG 6-18 Cast of characters from "Surprise Party" (Horse, Pig, Chicken, Sheep, Cow, Duck). All characters are made from items found at a dollar store.

Question: Can you figure out what they are made from?

Answer: The horse and cow are made from bone-shaped sponges with wooden and plastic spoons glued to them for rods. The pig is made from a bathtub back scrubber. The snout and the ears are pieces of a swimming pool noodle. The chicken is a feather duster with a small sponge cut and shaped for the head. The sheep body is a dog chew with a head made from a white plastic loofah. The duck is made from a cleaning brush, two dust pans, and three gloves (one stuffed for the body and two glued on as wings).

Content

This lesson can be used in units on days of the week, dates of the month, months of the year, and seasons.

Materials

Animal rod puppets or another type of puppets, block of Styrofoam, calendar or other prop to demonstrate concept presented

Note

The birthday party story allows the teacher to review days, dates, and months, and to discuss the experience of anticipation. The basic plot has a main character looking forward to her birthday at some time in the future. The character's friends are unclear about this concept, so she must review it over and over for their benefit. A birthday is used as the focal point of the lesson for two reasons. First, most children look forward to their birthday, and can identify with the main character in this respect. Second, unlike some other holidays or events, everyone has a different birthday. This fact allows the friends in the story to be confused, as it is not their birthday. The following lesson is an example of how these variables might be put together in one plot suggestion.

Preparation

Collect or make puppets. Practice the lesson without the children present.

Beginning the lesson

Seat the children in a circle or as desired. Introduce the puppet characters being used. In the example below they include Priscilla Pig, Sheep, Cow, Horse, Chicken, and Duck. As each rod puppet is introduced, stand it up in the Styrofoam block. Other puppets may be used if rod puppets are unavailable, and propped up where they can be seen and easily used.

Lesson with suggested dialogue

Teacher: **On Monday, Priscilla Pig went down to the old watering hole to meet her friends: the sheep,** the cow, the horse, the chicken, and the duck. Priscilla said to all her friends, "Friday is my birthday."

"That's nice," said the sheep.

"Wow!" said the cow.

"Hurray!" said the horse.

"Cheers!" said the chicken.

"Is it Friday yet?" asked the duck.

"No," said Priscilla. "Today is Monday!"

On Tuesday, Priscilla Pig met her friends at the old watering hole and she said, "Friday is my birthday."

"I know that," said the sheep.

"You told us," said the cow.

"Yes, I heard," said the horse.

"Cheers!" said the chicken.

"Is it Friday yet?" asked the duck.

"No," Priscilla said. "Today is Tuesday."

On Wednesday, Priscilla Pig met her friends at the old watering hole and she said, "Friday is my birthday."

"You said that on Monday," said the sheep.

"You said that on Tuesday," said the cow.

"We've heard it all before," said the horse.

"Cheers!" said the chicken.

"Is it Friday yet?" asked the duck.

"No," said Priscilla, "Today is Wednesday."

On Thursday, Priscilla Pig met her friends at the old watering hole and she said, "Friday is my birthday."

"You told us that on Monday," said the sheep.

"You told us that on Tuesday," said the cow.

"You told us that on Wednesday," said the horse.

"Cheers!" said the chicken.

"Is it Friday yet?" asked the duck.

"No," everyone said. "Today is Thursday."

Take all of the puppets out of the Styrofoam.

Teacher: On Friday, Priscilla Pig went down to the old watering hole and she couldn't find her friends anywhere. She called out to them. "Hello, Sheep . . . Hey, Cow . . . Horse, where are you? . . . Oh, Chicken . . . Yoohoo, Duck . . . It's Friday. . . . It's my birthday. . . . It's finally my birthday." But there was no answer.

Priscilla walked back to her house sadly, saying "Everyone forgot my birthday." When she got home, she opened her door and heard:

"Surprise! Happy Birthday!"

Put the puppets back in the Styrofoam one by one as they are named.

Teacher: And there in her living room were the sheep, the cow, the horse, and the chicken. They each had a present for her.

"I made you a straw hat on Monday," said the sheep.

"I drew you a birthday card on Tuesday," said the cow.

"I baked you a banana cake on Wednesday," said the horse.

"I picked these flowers for you on Thursday," said the chicken.

Just then the duck came rushing in all out of breath. "I just found out it's Friday, so I made a calendar for you."

Pull out the calendar.

Teacher:	It has the days of the week: Monday, Tuesday, Wednesday, Thursday, Friday . . . and look! There are two more days in the week. After Friday comes Saturday and after Saturday comes Sunday!

Suggested alternatives

- Priscilla goes to tell her friends it is her birthday, and gets lost. She is found when her friends look for her, knowing that it is her birthday and wanting to celebrate.

- Priscilla throws herself a birthday party and no one comes because they were confused about the day. When they discover their error, her friends throw her an un-birthday surprise party.

- The children in the class give Priscilla a party because her friends did not arrive as expected. Again, Priscilla's friends throw her an un-birthday surprise party.

- The characters may be altered to suit the teacher's puppet collection.

- Any one of several time concepts may be used: days, months, seasons, or dates. In the example, Priscilla Pig is looking forward to her birthday on Friday, so the class can review the names and order of the days of the week. Alternatively, she might be looking forward to her birthday on the fifth of the month. As her friends count down the days, they will be learning about both dates and ordinal numbers. Similarly, Priscilla might have a birthday in summer, and as her friends question it throughout the year, the students review the seasons, their names and qualities.

Follow-up

After performing "Surprise Party," leave the puppets out in a center for children to create "shows" with them any time.

Dealing with Fear

FIG 6-19 A ghost and a bat that could be used in a scary story.

Basis for lesson

Original activity

Character types

Animals, fantasy characters

Puppet use

Puppets putting on a play

Drama techniques

Using atmosphere as a stage (page 51), using fantasy character puppets (page 26)

Content

The "Dealing with Fear" lesson may be used when discussing feelings such as fear. It may be a part of a study on insects, bugs, or "creepy crawlies." For centers that recognize Halloween, it is a perfect way to include the scary without being scary.

Materials

Puppets (object puppets are fine) to represent things that typically scare preschoolers; a box for each puppet or object.

Preparation

Collect props to be used, and set up a haunted-house area in the classroom. Practice the lesson without the children present.

Beginning the lesson

Seat the children in a circle.

Lesson with suggested dialogue

Teacher: What kinds of things do you want to see in a haunted house?

Children may respond with such things as ghost, witch, bats, vampire, and skeleton. If the children do not suggest them, add snake, cricket, spider, mouse, or other common creatures that children are often afraid of.

Teacher: I have some of those things right here. I'm going to make our own haunted house out of them. Let's see . . . I'm going to put the spider in his box. The bat is in his box. Look—there are a lot of other boxes here, and we don't know what's in them.

Let the children see some of the objects so they are prepared for the surprises in the other boxes. Start the "tour" with a gesture, inviting the children to walk "into" the haunted house but patting their thighs with their hands while staying seated.

Teacher: Are you ready to walk over to the haunted puppet house? Let's walk with our hands on our legs. *(speaking softly)* It's getting dark. It's getting spooky. *(loudly)* Let's run!

Model "running" with your hands on your thighs.

Use the volume of the voice to test the waters. Warm the children up to the idea of going to a scary place. Monitor the children continually to make sure that no one is actually frightened. The more children participate by making noises and gestures, the less likely they are to be scared. Should a child indicate that they are truly scared, stop the activity to attend to that child. Never continue on and risk the individual child's emotional health to present the lesson to the rest of the class. If the class is ready, continue with the lesson.

Teacher: Let's go in. I'll open the door. *(Make the sound of a creaky door.)* Let's tiptoe in. Look! Here's a door. *(Hold up a box.)* Should we open it? *(whisper)* Okay, let's look.

Open the box slowly, but bring out the prop or puppet quickly. This should startle the children rather than scare them. Take the puppet to each child, alternating between slow and quick movements.

Teacher:	Can this cricket hurt us?

The children usually respond, "No!"

Teacher:	Right! Crickets can't hurt anyone, and besides, this is just a puppet. Shall we look behind another door?

The children usually respond, "Yes."

The teacher opens another box slowly.

Teacher:	Oh, no. This could be very scary.

Pull out the ghost and make ghostly sounds.

Teacher:	Oooooooo. Who can make a ghost sound? Great. I'll pass this ghost puppet around, and everyone can make a spooky ghost sound.

When the children are done, collect the ghost puppet.

Teacher:	Are there real ghosts?

The class will usually say, "No."

Teacher:	No, ghosts are just pretend, like my puppets are pretend.

This process of exploring a frightening item, then discussing its real qualities is repeated until all the props are discussed.

Teacher:	Time to walk back to school. Here we go, out the door. Should we run back to school? Yes? Okay, let's run.

Demonstrate jogging in place.

Teacher:	Whew! It's nice to be back in our good old classroom again, isn't it? You know, that haunted house didn't turn out to be so scary after all, did it?

Suggested alternatives

- The haunted house can easily become a lesson in ecology that also helps children become more familiar and friendly with an animal that might otherwise be scary. For example, upon finding bat puppets in the haunted house, distribute them among the students and let them eat mosquitoes. Classes requiring more control can eat mosquitoes while sitting in a circle on a rug; calmer classes can be invited to fly their bats around the room. The teacher would then explain how important bats are in the food chain, and how they help humans by eating mosquitoes. The teacher ends the segment by inviting students to thank the bats before they go back into their box.

- The haunted house is also an opportunity to teach about respect for nature. For instance, when the class finds a snake behind a "door," the teacher would take it out slowly and carefully. The teacher should not pretend to be afraid of the snake, or exhibit concern. Then, he should point out that while it is appropriate to touch and play with a puppet snake, it would be inappropriate and dangerous in the wild. Next, he can discuss some of the snake's behavior that is helpful to humans, such as eating mice that would otherwise overrun the community.

The Circus

FIG 6-20 Cast of characters for circus (Lion, Ringmaster, Clown with hoop for circus tricks).

Basis for lesson

Original activity

Character types

Animals, people

Puppet use

Puppet actors

Drama techniques

A non-plot-driven activity (page 67), nonverbal puppetry (page 46), using puppets that stimulate interest (page 58)

Content

The circus is a good lesson to introduce children to puppets, as it does not require speech from the puppeteer. This lesson works particularly well with children who have special needs, those who are nonverbal, or those who are working on their manual fine motor skills. It is also appropriate for units on the circus or animals.

Materials

Puppets that can represent circus performers, a rope, a hula hoop or other circle-shaped prop

Preparation

1)   Discuss and define a circus with the children. Read books about circuses, show video clips of a circus, bring in props from a circus (banner, cotton candy, poster, and so on).

2)   Tie a rope from the back of one chair to another.

3)   Practice the lesson without the children present.

Lesson with suggested dialogue

Begin by demonstrating a few circus tricks with puppets. Use an enthusiastic commentary.

Teacher: Presenting . . . the somersaulting lion! Let's see how many somersaults he can do. Let's count together! 1, 2, 3, 4, 5! Five somersaults! Let's clap for the lion. Hooray, lion!

Put the lion puppet away, and get out the clown. Balance the clown on top of the rope.

Teacher: Now presenting . . . on the high wire . . . the clown! Can the clown walk across the wire?

Speak softly and slowly to narrate the clown's first steps.

Teacher: Careful, careful, careful . . . *(Speak quickly and with urgency to describe the near disaster.)* Oops! Oh, no! He almost fell!

Repeat these steps until the clown makes it across the wire.

Teacher: Whew! He made it! Let's all clap for the clown!

Put away the clown, and get out an elephant puppet.

Teacher: Ladies and gentlemen, boys and girls . . . the elephant will now jump through the hoop! May I have a drum roll, please?

Demonstrate how the children can pat their thighs with their hands alternately to make a drum-roll sound.

Teacher: Now, the elephant will jump through the hoop!

Move the puppet through the hoop prop.

Teacher: Yes! The elephant jumped through the hoop! Let's all clap!

After presenting the acts, invite the children one by one to each manipulate a puppet to perform a circus act, while still acting as the ringmaster.

Suggested alternatives

- Change the characters, using whatever puppets are available. A horse may walk the tightrope, a dog may jump through the hoop, or a puppet of a human may do the acrobatics.

- Change the acts. If hand puppets are being used, the puppet might do a handstand. A bear might ride a bicycle, a dog might roll over, and the puppeteer might stick his finger in the lion's mouth.

- For large groups, let the children operate the puppets in groups of two or three to do the tricks.

- Another way to include large groups is to divide the class in half, and have each group present a different circus trick.

Butterfly in the Meadow

Basis for lesson

Original activity

Character type

Animals

Puppet use

Puppet actors

Drama techniques

A non-plot-driven activity (page 67), nonverbal puppetry (page 46), use of rod puppets (page 15)

Content

This lesson can be used in units on nature, color identification, and ecology. The motion used with rod puppets to flap wings is a fine motor skill important to emergent writing.

Materials

Enough butterfly puppets for each child, artificial flowers of different colors

Preparation

1) Place artificial flowers around the classroom.

2) Practice the lesson without the children present.

FIG 6-21 Katharine T. Manor holds a butterfly puppet.

Lesson with suggested dialogue

Show children how to make their butterflies fly safely around the room.

Teacher:	This is my butterfly puppet. Butterflies are very gentle. They never touch each other. They always land on flowers softly. They drink nectar from flowers, like this.

Land the butterfly puppet softly on an artificial flower, then make a slurping noise.

Teacher:	Then they fly to another flower. Here is a butterfly for each of you.

Pass out the puppets. While distributing them, continue to give directions on what to do with them.

Teacher:	Can you land the puppet gently on your head? Now fly high. Good. Now fly really high again. How low can you fly without touching the floor? Land the puppet gently on the floor.

Once each child has a puppet, they can begin to move around the room.

Teacher:	All around the room are flowers for the butterflies to drink from. Stand up and gently fly your butterfly and land on a red flower and drink the nectar.

Model these actions constantly as they are said.

Teacher:	Now fly to a yellow flower. Sometimes our butterflies are confused, and land on a color instead of a flower. Land on something orange. If you have a pink butterfly, land on a pink flower. If you have a yellow butterfly, land on a yellow flower. Great! Now fly your butterflies back to the circle and sit down. Land your puppets gently on the floor in front of you.

Collect the butterfly puppets.

Suggested alternatives

- Use another flying animal such as a bee, a bird, a bat, or a flying squirrel that jumps from tree to tree.

- Replace the flowers with items appropriate for the animals you are using. For example, nests for birds or fruit for bats.

- Use a variety of puppets and a variety of props to correlate with the puppets. Begin a sorting or classification lesson by discussing which animals would land on what items (a bird in a nest, a butterfly on a flower, a bee in a hive, a squirrel in a tree). Then ask the children to land their puppet on the appropriate item. Developmentally advanced children can then explore how the animals might overlap: the bee, as well as the butterfly, landing on the flower, and how squirrels have nests in trees like birds do.

CHAPTER 7

Making and Purchasing Puppets

LIKE THE LESSON plans in chapter 6, the directions in this chapter for making puppets should be freely altered to fit you and your classroom's needs. Sometimes, the most enduring, engaging, and exciting puppets are the result of experimentation. These puppets should be seen as prototypes that provide patterns and ideas for other kinds of puppets. For example, the fox puppet for *Mushroom in the Rain* could be made as a dog or a wolf, the mouse puppet could be redesigned to create almost any rodent, or the ant could become another kind of insect.

Most of the puppets included in this chapter are described as being made by an adult. Many times, you will choose to make the puppets rather than include the children, like when you are short on time and the benefits of having the children make them do not outweigh that concern. Likewise, if the specific kind of puppet you are making requires the use of razor blades, hot glue, and nonwashable paint, then you will not include the children. Many times, when a single puppet is being created (for example, a classroom assistant or specialty puppet) you will make it yourself because it is hard to have all of the students working on one puppet at the same time. Also, if a puppet with some durability is needed, perhaps because it will be handled often throughout the year, you may decide to make it on your own. There is more information about making puppets with children beginning on page 188.

Tips on Making Puppets

Materials that Make Excellent Puppets

Craft foam is nonabsorbent and comes in durable sheets of different thicknesses. It can be purchased in many bright colors at craft and fabric stores. Some of the various brand names are Fun Foam, Foamtastic, and Flex Foam.

Polyester foam is a sponge like foam used for upholstering. This kind of foam can also be found in pale-colored sponges at dollar stores. Foam or sponge balls can be found in various colors in toy stores and toy departments of discount stores, or can be purchased through the Oriental Trading Company (800-875-8480; www.orientaltrading.com).

You can change the color by painting the foam, if desired. One way to paint foam is to use a plastic bag. First, cut the foam into the desired shapes. Next, pour acrylic paint into a Ziploc bag. Add water to the paint and squeeze until the paint dissolves into the consistency of milk. Dip the foam pieces in water and add them to the bag. With the bag closed, manipulate the foam to ensure that the paint permeates the foam. Remove the foam and set out to drip dry without squeezing out the excess paint. Dry for about a week. Test to see if the foam is dry by squeezing it.

Another method is to use a paintbrush. Prepare the foam to its final form. For example, if you are making a puppet from a foam head, glue the ball to the stick and attach the nose and ears. Next, wet a portion of the foam with a plant mister or spray bottle before painting with an acrylic paint and brush. This method takes several days to dry.

Other kinds of balls, such as those used for the dog puppets on page 174, can also be used. Look for lightweight plastic baseballs or softballs in dollar stores, discount stores, or preschool supply catalogs. Tennis balls discarded by tennis clubs can be used after washing them in a washing machine with a strong detergent. Styrofoam balls are sold at craft stores.

FIG 7-1

Making Puppet Hair

It is easy and inexpensive to make hair to be glued on all types of puppet heads. Begin by wrapping a ½-inch-wide dowel about 10 inches long with yarn. Tie one end of the yarn loosely around one end of the dowel so it will slide off later. Wrap the dowel with yarn so that each loop fits closely to the one on either side of it and no wood shows. Keep the yarn fairly loose so it can slide off the dowel later. When the dowel is completely covered, run a bead of hot glue along the entire length of the dowel. [FIGURE 7-1] When the glue is cool, slip the yarn tube off the dowel. This should result in a 10-inch-long curl of yarn. [FIGURE 7-2] Use enough glue so the loops don't fall out as they come off the dowel. Then glue the curl of yarn to the puppet's head. [FIGURE 7-3] Several curls may be needed, depending on the size of the puppet's head. The size of the curls is determined by the width of the dowel used. For smaller puppets, use a thinner dowel to create smaller curls. Likewise, use a larger dowel to create curly hair for a larger puppet.

FIG 7-2

FIG 7-3

To achieve a brush cut or short Afro hairstyle, glue curls made with the above process to the puppet. Next, snip each loop. The effect results in little pieces of yarn sticking out of the puppet's head. Trim or "style" for the look you desire [FIGURE 7-4]

FIG 7-4

FIG 7-5

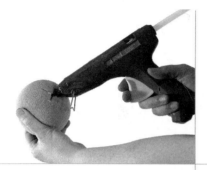

FIG 7-6

FIG 7-7

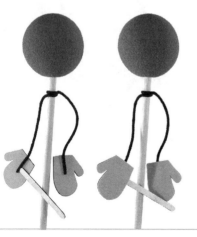

FIG 7-8   FIG 7-9

Directions for Making Simple Rod Puppets

(Such as those used for many puppet characters in "Mushroom in the Rain," pages 96–99, and "The Circus," pages 146–148.)

Materials

Hot glue gun and glue (not low-melt)

White glue such as Tacky (This can be used for some steps except where hot glue is specifically stated.)

Scissors with a point

Black, thin-tip permanent marker for drawing pupils

Sewing thread and needle or a sewing machine (optional)

Wooden dowel, ½ inch by 10 inches

Foam or sponge ball for head, 2½ inches or larger in diameter

Heavy twine or cord, 14 inches long

One small Popsicle stick

Material for body, two pieces about 12 by 9 inches

Scraps of felt or craft foam for hands and ears

Directions

Step 1:   Make a hole in the foam ball with scissors. [FIGURE 7-5]

Step 2:   Put hot glue into the hole and insert dowel. [FIGURES 7-6 and 7-7]

Step 3:   Glue heavy twine around the dowel, approximately 1 inch below the head.

Step 4:   Cut four hands out of felt or craft foam (see pattern in appendix, page 198) and glue one hand on each end of the twine. Glue a Popsicle stick to one hand. [FIGURE 7-8]

Step 5:   Glue the remaining hands in place, sandwiching the twine and Popsicle stick. [FIGURE 7-9]

Step 6:   Create the puppet body by draping and gluing fabric in place. Alternatively, cut out the body pattern (see appendix, page 198) and sew the edges with a ½-inch seam. The hem on the sleeves can be sewn or glued.

Step 7: Turn the body right-side out and slip it onto the puppet by pushing the dowel and the hands through the hole at the neck. Glue the body fabric to the dowel at the neck. Glue the sleeves to the hands, front and back. [FIGURE 7-10]

Step 8: At this point, the puppet can be an animal or a human. (Use steps 1 through 6 for Mouse, Rabbit, Fox, Frog, or Elephant.) If the puppet is to be a person, glue on hair. Glue on the eyes and make slits and insert the ears (see Baby Puppet, page 185). Use a bead or matching foam for a nose. Mouths can be drawn or glued onto the face.

FIG 7-10

Snouts for animals such as Mouse, Rabbit, Bear, Monkey, and Zebra

Step 1: Cut a foam ball in half with a scissors. This can be a color that matches or contrasts with the head.

Step 2: Cut a large pie-shaped piece out of the ball half as shown. [FIGURE 7-11]

Step 3: Hot glue the ball half together as shown. [FIGURE 7-12] Use masking tape to hold the foam together until the hot glue cools. [FIGURE 7-13]

Step 4: Glue the snout onto the head. Use masking tape to hold the foam together until the hot glue cools. [FIGURE 7-14]

Step 5: Mouths can be created with a marker, by gluing on felt or craft foam, or by cutting away a piece of foam from the snout. [FIGURE 7-15] FIGURE 7-16 shows three different sizes and shapes of foam snouts and cut mouths.

FIG 7-11

FIG 7-12

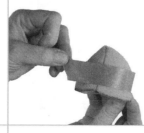
FIG 7-13

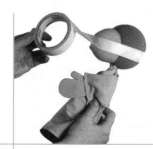
FIG 7-14

FIG 7-15

Step 6:   Add a bead, button, or pom-pom for a nose. Noses stay on better if you first snip away a little foam and then insert the nose (see Baby Puppet on page 185).

FIG 7-16

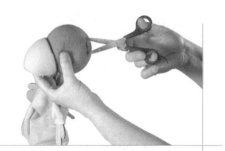

FIG 7-17

Animal ears

Step 1:   Cut a slit in the foam to insert the ears. [FIGURE 7-17] Different kinds of animals' ears are positioned in different locations on the head. For example, monkey ears and elephant ears are on the side of the head. Rabbit ears and tiger ears are on the top and back of the head.

Step 2:   Glue the ears into place. FIGURE 7-18 shows three different animals with distinct ears, noses, and eyes made from different materials.

FIG 7-18

Puppets for Lesson Plans in Chapter 6

Jamal and Mr. Bear

Materials for Mother Giraffe and Jamal

for the mother

4-inch yellow sponge ball
20-inch dowel, 1 inch in diameter

for Jamal

2½-inch yellow sponge ball
15-inch dowel, 1 inch in diameter

for both

12- by 18-inch sheet of yellow craft foam or two smaller sheets for
    necks, ears, hands, mouths, and horns.

14-inch piece of heavy twine
One Popsicle stick
Scraps of white craft foam for the eyes
Patterns for giraffe parts (appendix, page 201)

Directions

Step 1:   Follow steps 1, 2, and 3 for the simple rod puppets on page 156.

Step 2:   For Jamal, cover the dowel under the head with 5 inches of yellow craft foam to create a long neck. For the mother giraffe, cover the neck with 8 inches of yellow craft foam. Cover the neck with two more layers of craft foam to thicken it.

Step 3:   Wrap and glue the twine under the giraffes' necks. [FIGURE 7-19] Follow steps 4 through 8 on pages 156–157 to create the hands and bodies.

FIG 7-19

FIG 7-20

FIG 7-21

FIG 7-22

Step 4: Cut the mouth pieces from craft foam (see patterns in appendix, page 201). Cut a slightly curved slit for the lower mouth. Bend the foam so that the **V**-shaped cut closes [**FIGURE 7-20**], and glue it in place. [**FIGURE 7-21**]

Step 5: Cut a slightly curved slit for the upper jaw. Bend the foam so that the **V**-shaped cut closes and glue it in place.

Step 6: For Jamal, cover two dowel pieces, 1½- by ⅛-inch, with yellow craft foam. Cut slits in the top of the head and glue them in place. For the mother giraffe, cover the two dowel pieces, 1½- by ⅛-inch, with two layers of yellow craft foam and glue them in place.

Step 7: Cut the ear pieces from craft foam (see patterns in appendix, page 201). Cut ear slits on both sides of the head. Overlap the end of the foam ear [**FIGURE 7-22**] and glue the ears into the head.

Step 8: Glue on the eyes. [**FIGURE 7-23**]

Step 9: The tongue is optional (no pattern provided).

FIG 7-23

Elephant Puppet

Materials

Two sponge balls, 4 inches in diameter

10-inch dowel, ½ inch in diameter

14-inch piece of heavy twine

One Popsicle stick

Scraps of white craft foam for the eyes

Scraps of craft foam for the hands and ears

Patterns for elephant parts (appendix, page 200)

FIG 7-24

FIG 7-25

Directions

Step 1: Follow the directions for steps 1 through 8 on pages 156–157.

Step 2: Make two slices in the remaining 4-inch foam ball as shown in **FIGURE 7-24**.

Step 3: Trace the elephant trunk pattern (see appendix, page 200) onto one of the flat sides of the foam ball. [**FIGURE 7-25**]

Step 4: Cut out the shape drawn on the foam; next, trim into a rounded shape by snipping little pieces of foam until a trunk is created. [**FIGURE 7-26**] Glue trunk in place.

Step 5: Cut slits in the side of the head. Next, glue the ears (see pattern in appendix, page 200) in place, and then glue on the eyes. [**FIGURE 7-27**]

FIG 7-26

FIG 7-27

Ducky

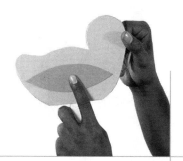

FIG 7-28

FIG 7-29

FIG 7-30

FIG 7-31

Materials for all puppets

Hot glue gun with glue (not low-melt glue; white glue optional unless hot glue is specified)

Thin-tip black permanent marker to draw in pupils and other features

Two ½-inch circles of white craft foam for each of the puppet's eyes

Two ½-inch wiggle eyes are optional

One large craft stick for each puppet (tongue depressor size)

Duck puppet

Materials

11- by 18-inch sheet of yellow craft foam

Small piece of orange craft foam for the beak and wing

Patterns for the Duck Puppet (appendix, pages 202 and 204)

Directions

Step 1:   Cut out the body parts from craft foam.

Step 2:   Glue the craft stick in place on the duck body.

Step 3:   Turn the puppet over and glue the other duck body on the back, "sandwiching" the craft stick. Glue the wings on both sides of the duck. [FIGURE 7-28]

Step 4:   Glue the lower beak to each side of the head. [FIGURE 7-29]

Step 5:   Glue the upper beak to each side of the head. [FIGURE 7-30]

Step 6:   Glue an eye to each side of the head.

Step 7:   Color in the pupil. [FIGURE 7-31]

Turtle Puppet

Additional materials

9- by 11-inch sheet of dark blue craft foam

9- by 11-inch sheet of light blue craft foam

Patterns for the Turtle Puppet (appendix, page 203)

Directions

Step 1:   Cut out the body parts from craft foam.

Step 2:   Glue the craft stick and two legs in place on the turtle body. [**FIGURE 7-32**]

Step 3:   Pinch the end of the neck so that it folds, and glue it together. [**FIGURE 7-33**]

Step 4:   Glue the tail, head, and remaining two legs in place on the body. The legs should not line up. [**FIGURE 7-34**]

Step 5:   Glue on the second body piece, "sandwiching" the craft stick and body parts. Glue the eyes in place. [**FIGURE 7-35**]

Step 6:   Draw the mouth, nose, and plates as shown, then color in the pupil. [**FIGURE 7-35**]

FIG 7-32

FIG 7-33

FIG 7-34

FIG 7-35

FIG 7-36

FIG 7-37

FIG 7-38

Beaver Puppet

Additional materials

11- by 18-inch sheet of red craft foam

Small piece of pink craft foam for snout

Very small piece of black craft foam for nose

Small piece of white craft foam for teeth

Patterns for the Beaver Puppet (appendix, pages 204–205)

Directions

Step 1: Cut out the body parts from craft foam.

Step 2: Glue the craft stick to the body. [FIGURE 7-36] Glue the legs and ears in place.

Step 3: Glue the tail in place on the craft stick. [FIGURE 7-37]

Step 4: Flip the puppet over and glue the arms, eyes, and snout in place. [FIGURE 7-38]

Step 5: Glue the nose and teeth onto the snout. Color in the pupils on the eyes and the lines on the legs. [FIGURE 7-39]

FIG 7-39

Frog Puppet

Additional materials

11- by 18-inch sheet of green craft foam (one sheet of dark green, one of light green)

Patterns for the Frog Puppet (appendix, page 206)

FIG 7-40

Directions

Step 1:   Cut out the body parts from craft foam.

Step 2:   Glue the craft stick in place on the body. [FIGURE 7-40]

Step 3:   Flip the puppet over and glue on the second body piece, "sandwiching" the craft stick.

Step 4:   Turn the puppet back-side up and glue the legs in place. [FIGURE 7-41]

Step 5:   Flip the puppet back to the front and glue the upper and lower snout on to the face. Glue the arms and eyes in place.

Step 6:   Color in the pupils and nostrils, and draw in the legs. [FIGURE 7-42]

FIG 7-41

FIG 7-42

Snake Puppet

Additional materials

Green knit fabric for skin, 10 by 48 inches in size

Needle and thread for sewing the Slinky to the fabric

Sewing machine (optional) for sewing the fabric body of the snake

Soft foam ball, 3 inches in diameter

Regular-size Slinky (metal only, not plastic)

Stuffing materials

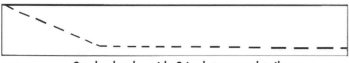

Snake body with 8-inch tapered tail

FIG 7-43

A 1½-inch dowel, 10 inches long

Hot glue gun and glue (not low-melt glue)

Two white circles of craft foam, ½ inch in diameter

Small piece of red craft foam for the tongue

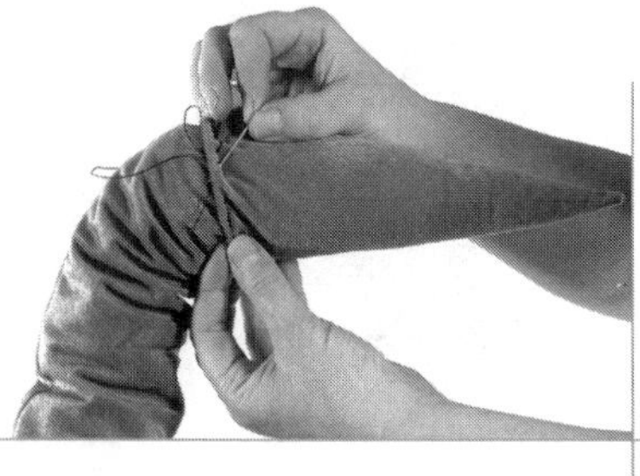

FIG 7-44

Directions

Step 1: Cut out snake body from the fabric. Fold in half the long way, wrong-side out.

Step 2: Sew the long side with a ½-inch seam allowance and taper the last 8 inches as shown. A sewing machine makes this step fast. [FIGURE 7-43]

Step 3: Trim the excess fabric and turn the snake body right-side out.

Step 4: Stuff the 8-inch tapered end with stuffing material.

Step 5: Drop the Slinky into the tube and stitch one end where the tapering stops. Stitch the other end of the slinky to the snake body opening. [FIGURES 7-44, 7-45]

Step 6: Make a hole in the foam ball with scissors for the dowel, as shown on page 158.

Step 7: Put hot glue into the hole and insert the dowel.

Step 8: Hot glue the fabric of the body around the foam ball. [FIGURE 7-46]

Step 9: Cut a slit, and glue in the tongue. Glue on the eyes and color in the snake's pupils. [FIGURE 7-47]

FIG 7-45

FIG 7-46

FIG 7-47

Shark Puppet

Additional materials

9- by 11-inch sheet of red craft foam

9- by 11-inch sheet of white craft foam

9- by 11-inch sheet of gray craft foam

One 6-inch pipe cleaner (any color)

Two white cardboard circles, 1¼ inch in diameter

One pair of brown jersey knit garden gloves

Hot glue gun and glue (not low-melt glue)

Thin-tip black permanent marker

Patterns for the Shark Puppet (appendix, page 207)

FIG 7-48

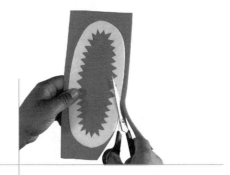

FIG 7-49

Directions

Step 1: Make an Anything Puppet as shown on page 183.

Step 2: Turn a left-handed glove inside out and put it on your right hand.

Step 3: Put a right-handed glove on top of the first glove so that you are wearing two gloves on the same hand.

Step 4: Slide the pipe cleaner eyes onto your gloved hand and glue them in place as shown. [FIGURE 7-48]

Step 5: Cut out the teeth from the white craft foam and glue them onto a red craft foam rectangle. Cut the rectangle into an oval shape to fit the teeth. [FIGURE 7-49]

Step 6: While wearing both gloves, put hot glue on the fingers and thumb of the glove and grab the folded shark mouth as shown. Do this step quickly to avoid overheating your hand. As soon as the mouth is in place on the glove, grab the fingers and thumb and carefully pull your hand out of the glove. [FIGURES 7-50, 7-51]

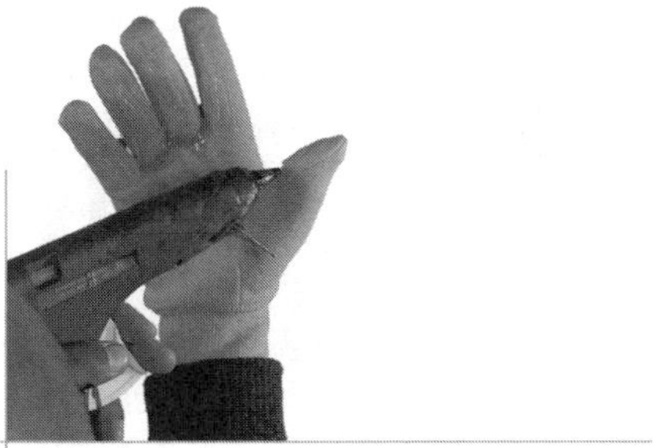

FIG 7-50

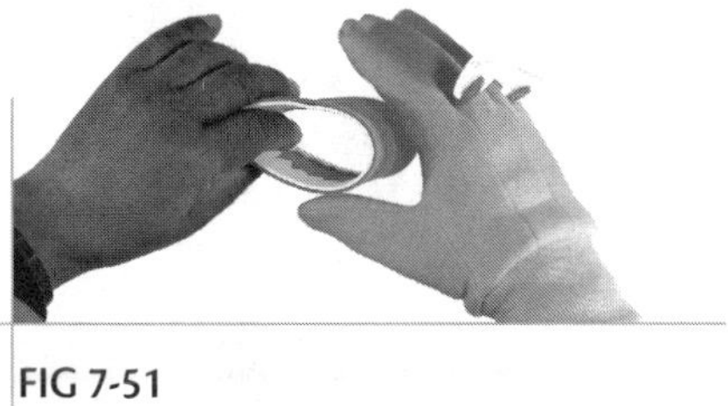

FIG 7-51

FIG 7-52

Step 7: Cut out the fin and tail. Glue on the back of the glove. Pull some fabric up from the glove and glue to either side of the fin to anchor it. [**FIGURES 7-52, 7-53**]

FIG 7-53

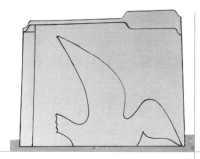

FIG 7-54

FIG 7-55

Pelican Puppet

Additional materials

Letter-size manila file folder

Stapler, scissors, tape

Glue (hot glue, white glue, or other paper glues)

Thin-tip black permanent marker

Patterns for the Pelican Puppet (appendix, page 208)

Directions

Step 1: Place the pattern on the fold of a letter-size manila folder. Trace the pattern and cut it out. [**FIGURE 7-54**]

Step 2: Create the wing flapper by cutting a strip ¾ inches from the edge of the folder as shown on the left side of **FIGURE 7-54**.

Step 3: Fold each wing in opposite directions and glue the body together. [**FIGURE 7-55**]

Step 4: Glue the wing flapper together from the fold to 4 inches from the fold.

Step 5: Fold each end of the wing flapper in opposite directions, and make another fold about ½ inch from the end. [**FIGURE 7-56**]

Step 6: Place the folded tips of the wing flapper in the position marked in the photo; glue, staple, or tape it in place. [**FIGURE 7-57**]

Step 7: Draw the beak and eyes. Pull down on the wing flapper to make the pelican fly. [**FIGURE 7-58**]

FIG 7-56

FIG 7-57

FIG 7-58

I Am Not a Dinosaur

Materials needed for Baby Pterodactyl

Letter-size manila file folder for each puppet needed

Stapler

Scissors

Tape

Glue (hot glue, white glue, or other paper glues)

Thin-tip black permanent marker

Pattern for Baby Pterodactyl (appendix, page 209)

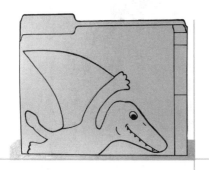

FIG 7-59

Directions for Baby Pterodactyl

Step 1:   Trace the pattern onto a file folder as shown. [FIGURE 7-59]

Step 2:   Follow the directions for the pelican puppet on page 168. FIGURE 7-60 shows the correct way to hold the puppet.

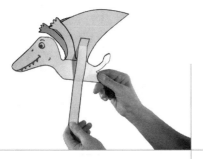

FIG 7-60

Materials needed for Mother Pterodactyl

Red poster board, 18 by 30 inches; or four red file folders

Patterns for Mother Pterodactyl (appendix, pages 210–211)

Directions for Mother Pterodactyl

Step 1:   Enlarge the four pattern pieces using a copying machine (enlarge each piece the same percentage). The choice of how large to make the mother puppet is not precise; anywhere from 30 to 40 percent larger than the baby works best.

Step 2:   Tape the enlarged pieces together to shape one Pterodactyl as shown. [FIGURE 7-61]

Step 3:   Trace the enlarged pattern onto red poster board that is folded in half, or glue four red file folders together and trace the enlarged pattern pieces onto the file folders.

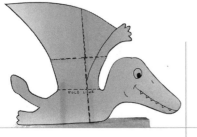

FIG 7-61

Mother Pterodactyl wing flapper

1 1/2″	fold		fold	1″
1 1/2″				

9 1/2″

FIG 7-62

Step 4:   Cut out the Mother Pterodactyl and assemble the puppet as you did the Baby Pterodactyl.

Step 5:   Fold down the wings and glue the body together just like the pelican on page 168.

Step 6:   The wing flapper is a little different from the pelican. Cut out four rectangles, 1½ by 9½ inches. [**FIGURE 7-62**] Create the wing flapper by gluing the rectangles together up to the 1½-inch fold. Attach the flapper up to the 1-inch fold to the wing. [**FIGURE 7-63**] Glue the other two rectangles on top of the first two in order to reinforce the wing flapper. **FIGURE 7-64** shows the Mother and Baby Pterodactyl.

FIG 7-63

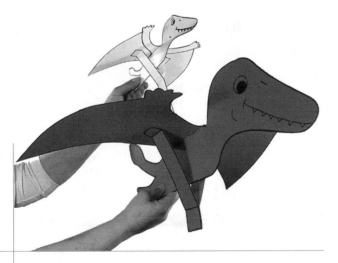

FIG 7-64

Small Brown Dog's Bad Remembering Day

Materials needed for all dogs

Scissors

Ballpoint pen or other permanent marking pen

Hot glue gun (White glue can be used on some steps, unless the instructions specifically call for hot glue.)

Black, white, or gray tube socks

Craft foam to match the socks for each dog

Patterns for the Dog Puppets (appendix, pages 212–215)

Red or pink craft foam for tongues

Wiggle eyes or eyes made from white craft foam with pupils drawn in permanent marker

1½- to 2-inch piece of cardboard tubing, 3 to 4 inches in diameter for each dog (You can get the tubing from rug stores or use mailing tubes. Cut them to size or use the inside of a masking tape roll. You also may use empty tuna cans. Be careful that there are no sharp edges, and cover the can with duct tape so it can be glued to the sock. Hot glue will stick to duct tape but not to tin cans.)

Materials needed for small brown dog (or other color as desired)

1½-inch dowel, 10 inches long, for each of the puppets (usually one for each child)

One adult-sized tube sock for each Small Brown Dog (Brown tube socks may not be possible to find, but all of the Small Dogs should be the same color, such as "Small Black Dogs" or "Small Gray Dogs.")

3- to 3½-inch ball for each small dog

Three 1-inch pom-poms for each dog (Choose the same color as the sock or a contrasting color.)

Small pink pom-pom or bead for the nose of each dog

Materials needed for the Seven Large Dogs (Tess the Terrier, Dan the Dalmatian, Bobby the Bulldog, Peaches the Poodle, Sid the Sausage Dog, Ralph the Rottweiler, and Alf the Alsatian)

Seven ½-inch dowels, 15 inches long

Seven adult-size tube socks (The color choice for each dog is optional, except Dan the Dalmatian needs a white sock.)

Seven balls ranging from 3 to 5 inches (Choose a variety of sizes; for example, Bobby the Bulldog may be made with a 5-inch ball and Dan may be made with a 3-inch ball.)

Twenty-one pom-poms ranging in size from 1 to 2 inches (Three pom-poms are needed for each dog snout. Choose larger pom-poms for larger heads. The colors can either match or contrast with the sock.)

Seven beads or small pom-poms for noses (Choose an appropriate size and color for each dog.)

FIG 7-65

FIG 7-66

Doggy details

Tess the Terrier needs four extra pom-poms for sideburns.

Peaches the Poodle needs ten 1-inch pom-poms, one ½-inch pom-pom, and three 2-inch pom-poms.

Dan the Dalmatian needs small black circles of craft foam to glue on for spots on the snout, and a black permanent marker to make spots on the rest of the body.

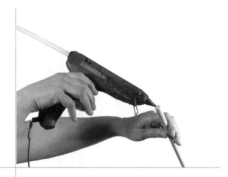

FIG 7-67

Directions for making all of the dogs (except the finger puppet Charlie)

Step 1: Using a sharp knife, poke a hole into a ball. The hole should be just big enough to insert the end of a scissors.

Step 2: Cut out a hole just big enough to insert the ½-inch dowel. [FIGURE 7-65] Push the dowel into the hole to test the size before proceeding. If the hole is too big the dowel cannot be glued in place. If a tennis ball is used, this step will be done with a sharp knife. It is not necessary to remove the rubber from the tennis ball;

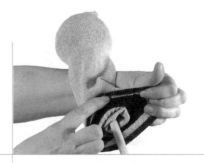

FIG 7-68

FIG 7-69

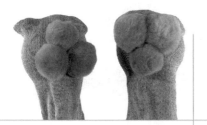

FIG 7-70

FIG 7-71

simply gouge the ball with the knife enough to insert the ½-inch dowel.

Step 3: Put a dab of hot glue onto the end of the dowel. [**FIGURE 7-66**]

Step 4: Push the dowel into the hole. Use hot glue to attach the dowel to the ball. [**FIGURE 7-67**]

Step 5: Push the ball and the dowel into a tube sock.

Step 6: Cut the sock to the desired length and tuck the raw edge inside as if to fold up a hem. [**FIGURE 7-68**] The Small Brown Dog needs a very short sock, while the other socks are much longer.

Step 7: Insert the cardboard roller into the end of the sock.

Step 8: Glue the roller to the turned-up sock. [**FIGURE 7-69**]

Step 9: The three pom-poms for the snout can be glued in two different shapes. Choose either shape as shown for each dog. [**FIGURE 7-70**]

Step 10: Noses, tongues, and eyes can be glued on as shown. [**FIGURE 7-71**] The Small Brown Dog has a patch of craft foam glued behind one eye.

Step 11: Ears: Tess the Terrier, Alf the Alsatian, Dan the Dalmatian, and Charlie the Chihuahua all have their ears glued on to the back and side of the head. Dan the Dalmatian's ears have the tips glued in a bent shape. [**FIGURE 7-72**] Ralph the Rottweiler, Sid the Sausage Dog, and Peaches the Poodle have their ears glued on the sides of their heads. [**FIGURE 7-73**] Peaches the Poodle has pom-poms glued onto her ears. Bobby the

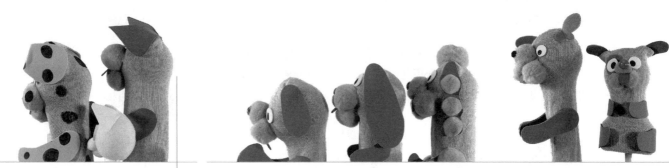

FIG 7-72   **FIG 7-73**   **FIG 7-74**

Bulldog and the Small Brown Dog have small ears that stick up. They are glued to the top and side of the head. [FIGURE 7-74]

Step 12: Tess the Terrier has pom-poms glued on each side of the face; the pom-poms are trimmed with a scissors so that they don't look so round. [FIGURE 7-75]

Step 13: The front legs and the back legs of each breed vary in size, but they are all positioned on the sides. [FIGURE 7-76]

Step 14: Peaches the Poodle has pom-poms glued on her ears, legs, tail, and the top of her head. [FIGURE 7-77]

Step 15: Most of the dogs' tails are glued flat in the middle of the lower backside of the puppet. [FIGURE 7-78] Alf the Alsatian's tail is glued by pinching the sock around the tail so that the tail sticks out. [FIGURE 7-79]

Step 16: Glue black dots on the snout and draw black dots with a marker all over Dan the Dalmatian. [FIGURE 7-80]

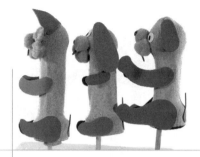

FIG 7-75

FIG 7-76

FIG 7-77

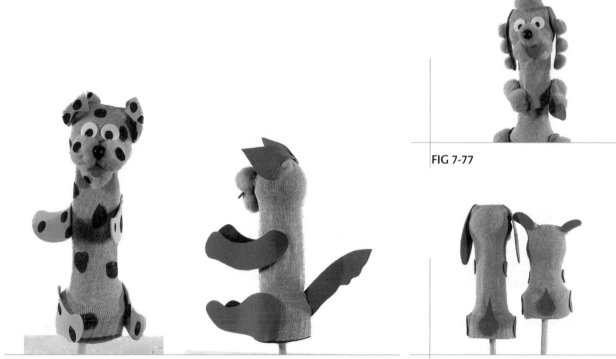

FIG 7-80

FIG 7-79

FIG 7-78

FIG 7-81

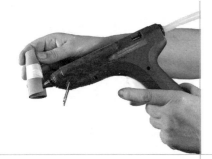

FIG 7-82

FIG 7-83

FIG 7-84

Charlie the Chihuahua

Materials

Small foam ball of any color, 2 to 2½ inches

Craft foam rectangle 2½ by 4½ inches (The color should match the foam ball as closely as possible.)

Three ½-inch pom-poms for snout (Choose a matching or contrasting color.)

Very small bead or pom-pom for nose

Two small wiggle eyes

Craft foam for the tail, legs, and ears (Choose a matching or contrasting color.)

Red or pink craft foam for tongue

Directions

Step 1: Make a finger tube around your finger from the 2½- by 3½-inch piece of craft foam and secure it with masking tape. [FIGURE 7-81]

Step 2: With the masking tape in place, hot glue the ends of the tube. [FIGURE 7-82]

Step 3: Remove the masking tape and finish gluing the tube closed along the middle seam.

Step 4: Cut a hole in the foam ball big enough for the finger tube. [FIGURE 7-83] Snip with a scissors and pull out the excess foam.

Step 5: Put hot glue into the hole in the foam ball and insert the finger tube. [FIGURE 7-84]

Step 6: Glue on the body parts in the same way that the other dogs are created, starting from the previous step 9. [FIGURE 7-85]

FIG 7-85

Mushroom in the Rain

General directions useful in making the Mouse, Zebra, and Rabbit puppets can be found in the section on making Simple Rod Puppets, pages 156–158.

Frog Puppet

FIG 7-86

Materials

Two sponge balls, 2½ inches in diameter

10-inch long dowel, 1½ inches in diameter

14-inch piece of heavy twine or cord

One Popsicle stick

Scraps of craft foam for hands and ears

Two 1½-inch black buttons for eyes

FIG 7-87

Directions

Step 1: Follow steps 1 through 8 on pages 156–157.

Step 2: Cut a foam ball in half and in half again, creating this shape. [FIGURE 7-86]

Step 3: Looking at one of the flat sides you just created, draw a triangle or pie shape, then cut away the foam. Repeat with the second quarter sphere. [FIGURE 7-87]

Step 4: Glue both pieces together and glue them to the head. [FIGURE 7-88]

Step 5: Cut out the mouth. Glue the button eyes on the head and snip holes for the nose. [FIGURE 7-89]

FIG 7-88

FIG 7-89

FIG 7-90

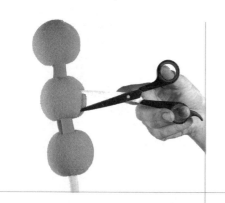

FIG 7-91

FIG 7-92

Red Ant

Materials

10-inch dowel, ½ inch in diameter

Three 2½-inch red sponge balls

One 9- by 11-inch sheet of red craft foam

Two pink pipe cleaners

Two red pipe cleaners

Scraps of white craft foam for the eyes

2 feet of heavy twine or sash cord cut into 4-inch pieces

Directions

Step 1: Follow steps 1, 2, and 3 on page 156.

Step 2: Cut holes through two more balls that are the same size as the head and slide them onto the dowel. Then glue the balls in place as shown in **FIGURE 7-90**.

Step 3: Cut two ½- by 3½-inch strips of red craft foam.

Step 4: Glue one strip around the dowel under the top ball. Glue the second piece of craft foam around the dowel under the middle ball. [**FIGURE 7-91**]

Step 5: Cut heavy twine into six 4-inch pieces.

Step 6: Cut two slits into the sides of the center foam ball. [**FIGURE 7-91**]

Step 7: Cut slits in the top of the head. [**FIGURE 7-92**]

Step 8: Insert three pieces of twine into each slit in the center ball, and glue them into place. Cut out the twelve craft foam pieces for the feet (see pattern on page 200). Glue the two feet on to the end of each piece of twine, "sandwiching" the twine. Twist the pink and the red pipe cleaners together like candy canes. Glue the antennae in place. [**FIGURE 7-93**]

Step 9: Glue the eyes into place. [**FIGURE 7-94**]

FIG 7-93

FIG 7-94

FIG 7-95

FIG 7-96

FIG 7-97

FIG 7-98

Fox

Materials

2½-inch sponge ball

10-inch dowel, 1½ inch in diameter

14-inch piece of heavy twine

One Popsicle stick

Scraps of white craft foam for the eyes and teeth (optional)

Scraps of craft foam for hands, ears, and snout

Patterns for snout and jaw (appendix, page 199)

Directions

Step 1: Follow steps 1 through 8 on pages 156–157

Step 2: Cut a curved slit for the snout. Glue the snout into place. [FIGURE 7-95]

Step 3: Cut a curved slit for the jaw and glue the jaw in place. [FIGURE 7-96]

Step 4: Glue a black bead inside the end of the snout so that only half of the bead shows. [FIGURE 7-97]

Step 5: Cut teeth from white foam (no pattern is provided) and glue in place. [FIGURE 7-98]

Step 6: Cut a curved slit in the head for the ears and glue in place. [FIGURE 7-99]

Step 7: (optional) Cut a slit in the mouth and glue in a tongue (no pattern provided).

FIG 7-99

Bird

Materials

18- by 12-inch sheet of craft foam

2½-inch sponge ball

12-inch dowel, ½ inch in diameter

Scraps of white craft foam for the eyes

Patterns for bird parts (appendix, pages 200 and 216)

FIG 7-100

Directions

Step 1:   Follow steps 1, 2, and 3 on page 156.

Step 2:   Cut a slit for the beak and for the head crest. Glue the beak and head crest in place.

Step 3:   Wrap a strip of craft foam around the dowel, under the head. [FIGURE 7-100]

Step 4:   Fold a piece of paper in half. Lay the wing pattern in place, straight edge along the fold. Cut out the pattern. Trace the pattern onto the craft foam and cut out.

Step 5:   Glue the wings to the dowel. Glue the tail in place on the back of the wings. [FIGURE 7-101]

Step 6:   Glue the body onto the bird, "sand-wiching" the dowel between the body and the wings.

Step 7:   Glue the eyes in place. [FIGURE 7-102]

FIG 7-101

FIG 7-102

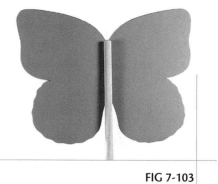

FIG 7-103

Butterfly

Materials

9- by 11-inch sheet of brightly colored craft foam

Small piece of black or brown craft foam

12-inch black or brown pipe cleaner

18-inch dowel, ½ inch in diameter

Directions

Step 1: Fold a piece of paper in half. Lay the butterfly pattern (page 217) in place, straight edge along the fold. Trace the pattern onto the craft foam and then cut out the butterfly.

Step 2: Glue the wings to the dowel. [FIGURE 7-103]

Step 3: Shape the pipe cleaner into antennae and glue them to the body.

Step 4: Glue the body onto the dowel, "sandwiching" the dowel between the wings and the body. [FIGURE 7-104]

FIG 7-104

The Anything Puppet

Materials

Pipe cleaner

White tagboard

Glue

Black marker or black paper

Scissors

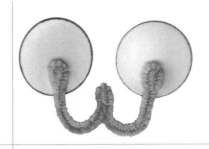

FIG 7-105

FIG 7-106

Directions

Step 1: Cut two 1¼-inch circles out of white tagboard.

Step 2: Bend a 6-inch piece of pipe cleaner into the size and shape of **FIGURE 7-105**. Glue the pipe cleaner ends to the circles as shown.

Step 3: Turn the puppet over and draw pupils or cut out a black circle about the size of a penny, and glue in place. **[FIGURE 7-106]**

Step 4: Line up the puppet at the tips of fingers as shown. **[FIGURE 7-107]**

Step 5: Slide the puppet onto the fingers as far as it will go. **[FIGURE 7-108]**

FIG 7-107

FIG 7-109

FIG 7-110

FIG 7-108

Step 6: Look at your puppet and straighten the eyes if necessary, so that it looks like it can see. [FIGURE 7-109]

Step 7: The pipe cleaner can be bent for effects. [FIGURE 7-110]

Step 8: The Anything Puppet can be dressed up with simple hats and scarves. [FIGURES 7-111, 7-112]

FIG 7-111

FIG 7-112

The Baby Puppet

Materials

Use the list of general materials needed for simple rod puppets on page 156

Soft foam ball (Nerf-type ball), 4 inches in diameter

One 10-inch dowel, ½ inch in diameter

Popsicle stick

16-inch piece of heavy twine or cord

Scraps of craft foam that match the color of the head (for ears and hands)

Two ¼-inch beads that are an appropriate color for noses

Scraps of white craft foam for eyes or other appropriate eyes (remember babies have large eyes compared to their heads)

One 10- by 19-inch piece of fabric for a baby blanket

Ribbon for a bow (optional)

FIG 7-113

FIG 7-114

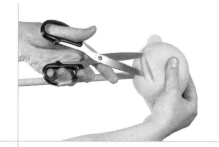

FIG 7-115

Directions

Step 1:   Follow steps 1 and 2 on page 156.

Step 2:   Cut ear slits in each side of the foam ball.

Step 3:   Cut two small ears from craft foam and glue them into the ear slits. [FIGURE 7-113]

Step 4:   Create the frown and smile by cutting the ball at an angle. Angle the scissors up for the frown. [FIGURE 7-114] Angle the scissors down for the smile. [FIGURE 7-115]

Step 5:   Make a second parallel cut with the scissors at the same angle as the first cut. This will enlarge the mouth.

Step 6:   Pull the excess foam out from each mouth with your fingers. [FIGURE 7-116]

FIG 7-116

FIG 7-117

Step 7: Snip a bead-size hole in each face for the nose. [FIGURE 7-117]

Step 8: Put hot glue in the holes and insert beads on each side of the foam ball. [FIGURE 7-118]

Step 9: Glue the eyes on each face. Remember that babies have large eyes that are close to the mouth and nose. [FIGURE 7-119]

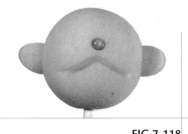

FIG 7-118

FIG 7-119

FIG 7-120

Step 10: Sew a tube from a 10- by 19-inch piece of fabric and hem both ends. [FIGURE 7-120]

Step 11: Cut a 16-inch piece of cord or heavy twine. Tie a loose knot around the head stick and then slide it off the loop. [FIGURE 7-121]

Step 12: Hot glue or sew the knot into the seam 1½ inches from one end. [FIGURE 7-122]

Step 13: Glue or sew the seam allowance flat. If you are using hot glue, add extra hot glue to the knot.

Step 14: Turn the tube right-side out and insert the baby's head stick through the loop in the cord. [FIGURE 7-123] Put the stick through the fabric tube.

Step 15: Attach the hands and Popsicle stick as shown in steps 4, 5, and 6 on page 156.

Step 16: Glue or sew the fabric tube closed on each side of the head. [FIGURE 7-124] Do not glue fabric to the head, head stick, or hands and hand cords.

Step 17: Add a bow or other decorations as desired.

Step 18: The puppet is operated by turning the stick inside the fabric from one face to the other when the baby cries. [FIGURE 7-125] Hang on to the fabric from the outside while the head is turning.

FIG 7-121

FIG 7-122

FIG 7-123

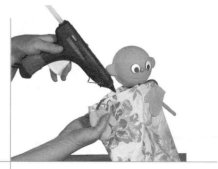

FIG 7-124

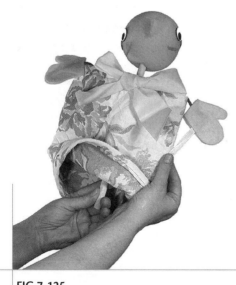

FIG 7-125

Children Making Puppets

Puppet making is truly a developmentally appropriate activity. It is age appropriate in that young children are capable of making simple puppets and it is individually appropriate in that a child may participate on whatever level she can. For example, once the teacher has chosen to make a puppet that suits the abilities of her class, each child may come up with a variation that reflects her own physical and mental development as well as her own tastes.

The benefits of making puppets with children are myriad. They include the following:

- Supporting kinesthetically inclined children with a project that can be touched and felt

- Giving children opportunities to exercise fine motor skills

- Encouraging students' creativity

- Providing students with a puppet that can be used at home and discussed with parents

- Providing students with an automatically successful activity that can boost self-esteem

- Giving the children ownership of the puppet show and allowing children to feel pride in their combined accomplishment

The flexibility in making puppets does not end with developmental issues; children can make a wide variety of puppets to serve a wide variety of uses in the classroom. In fact, children can help with making almost any type of puppet.

Finger Puppets	Students can help decorate the fingers of an inexpensive white cotton glove to make their own puppet.
Hand Puppets	Paper bag puppets (in which the bottom of a lunch sack is folded over to make a mouth) have long been in use in classrooms.
Rod Puppets	Anything on a stick can be a rod puppet. Students may decorate flat, cardboard fans (such as those found in some churches) to make rod puppets.
Shadow Puppets	Students can help draw, trace, and cut shapes to be used as shadow puppets.
Marionettes	Perhaps the most difficult puppet to make and manipulate, this may be the one puppet that is developmentally inappropriate for young children to make or use. (However, they are excellent for young children to watch!)
Object Puppets	Children may be invited to find items around the classroom to represent characters in a planned or impromptu puppet play.
Hat Puppets	Students can use white glue, felt shapes, and markers to create puppets from painters' hats.

Making puppets with children is often recognized as an excellent art project that promotes creativity. However, all too often the teacher stops there, unsure of how to use the puppets after they have been created. While this book encourages adults to make puppets with children, its focus is on how they are to be used. Because we devote little time to making puppets with children, those who wish to further explore this possibility may want to consult *The Muppets Make Puppets!/Book and Puppet Kit: How to Make Puppets Out of All Kinds of Stuff Around Your House* by Cheryl Henson.

When making puppets with children, decide beforehand how to model what will be made. An elaborate, teacher-made puppet often inspires younger children in the preoperational developmental stage. In this case, the children make their own puppets, are pleased with the result, and remain unaware that their creation is any different from the one you modeled. On the other hand, adult-made puppets often frustrate older children who are reaching the concrete developmental stage. They feel that their puppet does not look like and is not as good as the one you made. They become frustrated and dissatisfied with their own work. In this situation it is best to show the children the basics of how the puppet will be assembled (for example, how to insert a rod body onto a ball head) and let the materials inspire the children's creations. The wider the variety of textures, colors, and applications provided by the materials, the wider the variety of puppet results. In sum, you should assess your class and decide how to best promote creativity when modeling an already-made puppet. The child with advanced fine motor skills may braid yarn for hair on her puppet, while another child may simply use a crayon to color on the hair.

Use your own discretion regarding safety issues when creating puppets. Items not ordinarily allowed, such as sharp-tipped scissors and hot-glue guns, should be avoided, but with these exceptions children can be invited to make any kind of puppet with any available materials.

On the next page, you will find instructions for children making a mouth puppet using a paper plate. Just as adults should try new things when creating puppets, children should be encouraged to experiment as well. The supplies available will dictate some of this creativity, but new ideas in construction and design should be welcomed too. Have the children make as much of the puppet as they are capable of. Help them enough so they don't get frustrated, but let the final product truly belong to the child.

Paper Plate Puppet

Materials

One paper plate per child (either a 9-inch dinner plate or a 6-inch dessert plate)

Circle stencil such as a jar lid, cardboard circle, or small plate about 4 inches in diameter

One sock per child

Staplers

Pencils, markers, or crayons

Construction paper or fun foam

Optional: additional decorative items, such as sequins, lace, wallpaper samples, fabric swatches

Optional: adhesives to use with the decorative items, such as glue, paste, or tape

Directions

Have the children help with these steps in any way they can.

Step 1: Using the stencil, trace a circle about 1½ inches from the edge of the plate as shown. A 2¾-inch-diameter hole is necessary for small hands. A 3½-inch-diameter hole is necessary for large hands.

Step 2: Cut around the circle to make a hole.

Step 3: Cut off the end of the sock between 2 and 3 inches from the toe of the sock.

Step 4: The eating side of the plate is the backside of the puppet. For a small-mouthed character, staple the toe end of the sock over the hole in the paper plate, stretching the cut end around the edges of the hole. Place staples in the same positions as points on a compass, starting with north, then south, then east, then west, finally adding staples in between. The plate may need to be gently folded to fit into the stapler. The sock should

FIG 7-126

FIG 7-127

FIG 7-128

FIG 7-129

FIG 7-130

look like a bump or a pocket sticking out from the lower side of the plate. This will be the puppet's mouth. For a long-nosed character, use the upper tube end of the sock, and staple as indicated above. Refer to **FIGURES 7-126 and 7-127** for guidance.

Finishing the Puppets

Step 1: Hold up a sample of the stapled plates and socks. Put four fingers into the pocket [**FIGURE 7-128**] created by the sock and explain that this will be a puppet. Ask the children what kind of puppet it should be. Then ask what else it needs in order to really look like the chosen animal. Let the children volunteer answers, such as eyes, tongue, ears, whiskers, and so forth.

Step 2: Ask the children to raise their hands if they will be making a different kind of animal from the one the teacher is making. Ask questions about what features the child will add and what materials he will use to make them. [**FIGURES 7-129, 7-130**]

Step 3: After eliciting several ideas of puppet types and how they might be made, review the materials available to the children along with any classroom rules about using them.

Let the children create their puppets while the adults circulate to answer questions. Comment on the children's ingenuity, or solve problems if necessary.

If glue was used, allow time for drying and ask the children to write their names on the inside of their puppets.

Using the Puppets

The puppets made by the children can be used in many of the lesson plans included in this book. *Jamal and Mr. Bear* requires only a bear; the rest of the animals can be suggested by the children's imaginations. Other lesson plans can be changed; for example, making the three little pigs into the three little kitties and the big bad dog. If you want to use a book with the characters as written, give the children a list of the characters and let them pick the one they want to make. In this case, a puppet enactment of *Mushroom in the Rain* might end up with three ants, two mice, and four foxes. The children who have the same character would all manipulate their puppets at the same time and say their lines as an ensemble.

Uses for child-made puppets are by no means limited to the lesson plans in this book. Make up your own lesson, let the children create their own story, or use their puppets as task puppets.

Purchasing Puppets

If it is not preferable to make puppets, there are many good puppets available for purchase. Some are made for children's hands, and others are adult sized. It is important that the puppet is the appropriate size for the user. Children's puppets should not be too big to manipulate and adults should not try to use a puppet that is too small. If a puppet is uncomfortable it will be used infrequently. Uncomfortable puppets are never worth the cost.

Many store-bought puppets can be greatly improved by gluing cardboard into the mouths so that they close properly. Since a puppeteer's hand gets wet with perspiration quickly, a moisture barrier can be created by hot gluing three layers of cardboard together, then covering it entirely with duct tape. Never hesitate to glue, staple, or sew commercially produced puppets to improve them for your specific needs.

Puppets might be purchased in two circumstances. First, you may find a puppet you like and buy it although you have no particular use for it. Second, you may find a specific book or topic you want to use puppets for and look for a particular type of puppet to satisfy the need. In the first case, you have several options. You might put a child-sized puppet in a center for free choice time, or you share your purchase with the children and explain why you like the puppet. Bring the children into the play by asking them what kind of voice the puppet should

FIG 7-131

have, where the puppet lives, why it might come to visit the classroom, and other questions pertaining to how it might be used. Through this process, the children decide what the puppet's function will be in the classroom. You can then operate the puppet as dictated by the students, or let the students operate it during small group time. Alternatively, you may simply hold on to the puppet, waiting for the right subject, book, song, or event to introduce it.

When you look for a particular puppet, there are several resources to explore. Puppets are available in toy and teaching stores, or they can be ordered through educational supply catalogs, toy catalogs, and from puppet companies. There are a number of resources on the Internet as well.

If you can't find a particular puppet, consider altering a plush animal to suit your needs. While each stuffed animal is different, making it impossible to give precise instructions on how this can be done, there are a few tips that will make the process easier.

To make a hand puppet, first look at the stuffed animal and determine where the puppeteer's hand will fit in. Would there be a place to insert the hand? Where will the fingers go? How would the puppet move? Some figures such as teddy bears have heads that are too flat, and do not have enough space for a puppeteer's hand between the nose and the back of the head. These types of stuffed animals must be rejected. Next, look at the construction of the stuffed animal and think about what stuffing will have to be removed, and what will have to stay in the puppet to maintain the shape. If it is clear that there is no room for a hand in the toy, or that removing the stuffing would be impossible, another toy animal should be considered. A stuffed animal with plastic eyes or pieces that might easily fall out from the inside should also be dismissed. With these precautions aside, many stuffed animals can be converted into puppets with creativity. [FIGURE 7-131]

Small, stuffed creatures can also be turned into rod puppets. To do this, make a hole in the animal's bottom just big enough for a dowel ½ inch to ¾ inch in diameter. Push the dowel into the puppet several inches, working the rod into the stuffing. If you are using small animals filled with beans, the dowel must extend into the head. To animate an arm, make a small slit in a hand or paw and insert a Popsicle stick. Glue both sticks in place with hot glue, white glue, or carpenter's glue. [FIGURE 7-132]

FIG 7-132

Appendix: Puppet Patterns

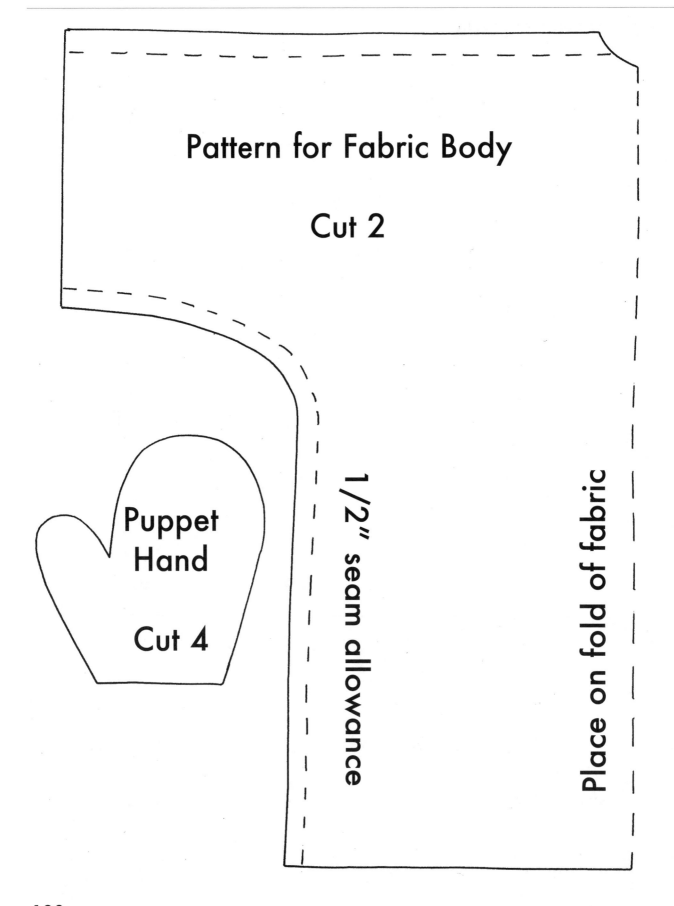

Pattern for Fabric Body

Cut 2

Puppet Hand

Cut 4

1/2" seam allowance

Place on fold of fabric

Pattern for rabbit and fox ears

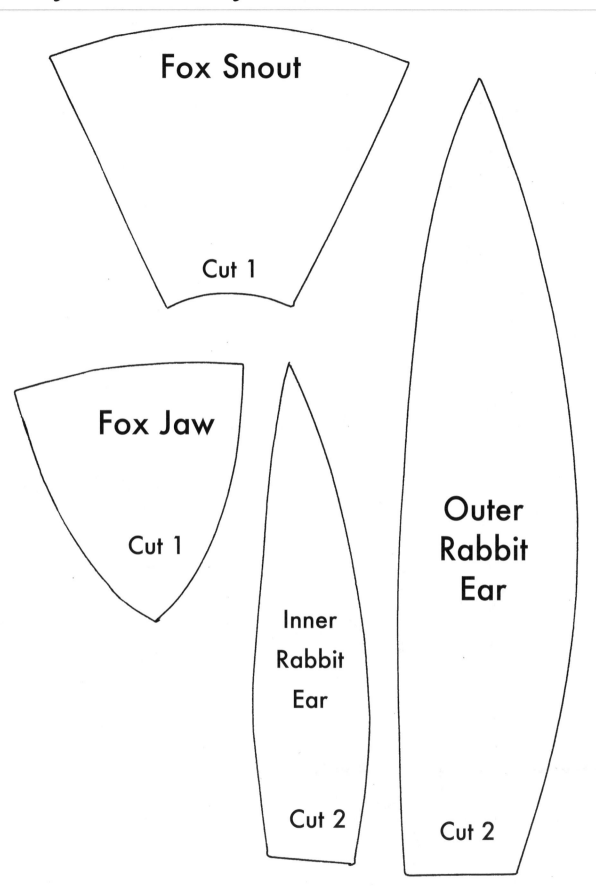

Fox Snout

Cut 1

Fox Jaw

Cut 1

Inner Rabbit Ear

Cut 2

Outer Rabbit Ear

Cut 2

Pattern for miscellaneous parts

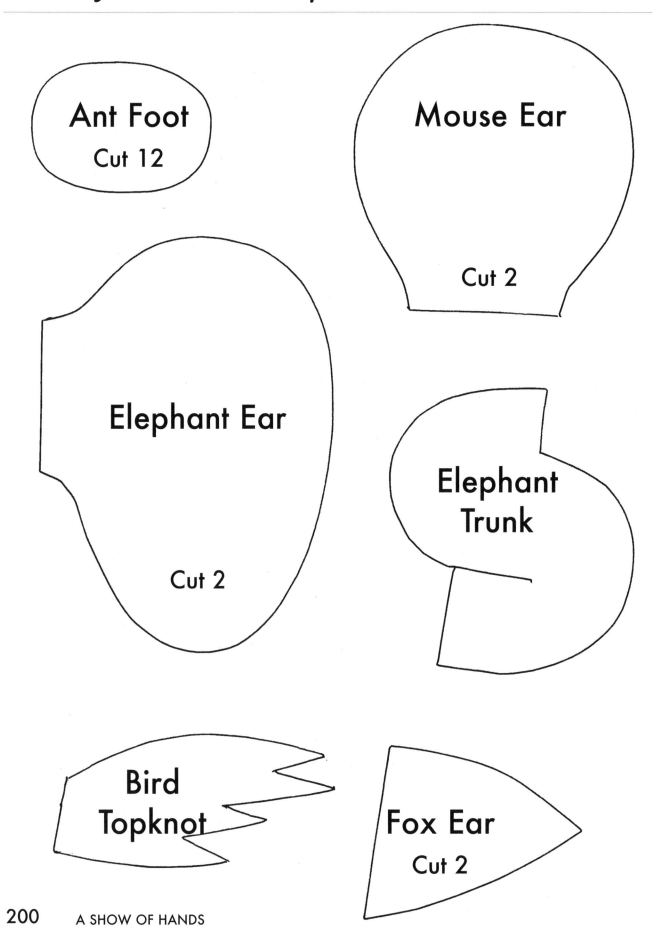

Ant Foot
Cut 12

Mouse Ear
Cut 2

Elephant Ear
Cut 2

Elephant Trunk

Bird Topknot

Fox Ear
Cut 2

Pattern for giraffe parts

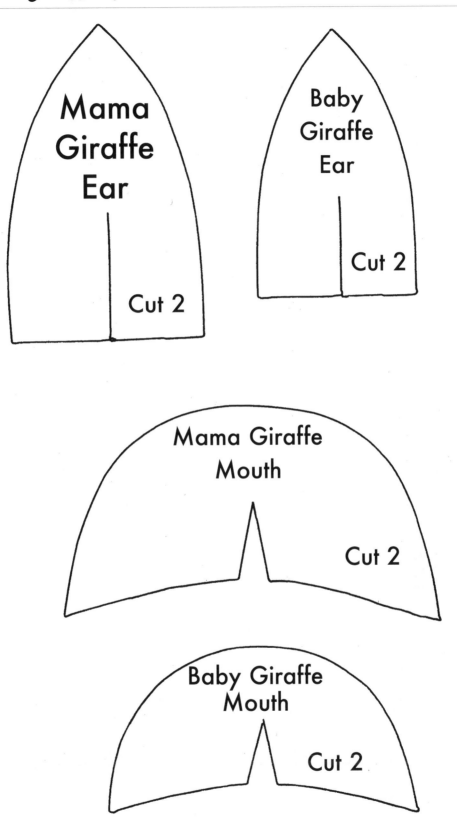

Mama
Giraffe
Ear

Cut 2

Baby
Giraffe
Ear

Cut 2

Mama Giraffe
Mouth

Cut 2

Baby Giraffe
Mouth

Cut 2

Pattern for duck and body parts

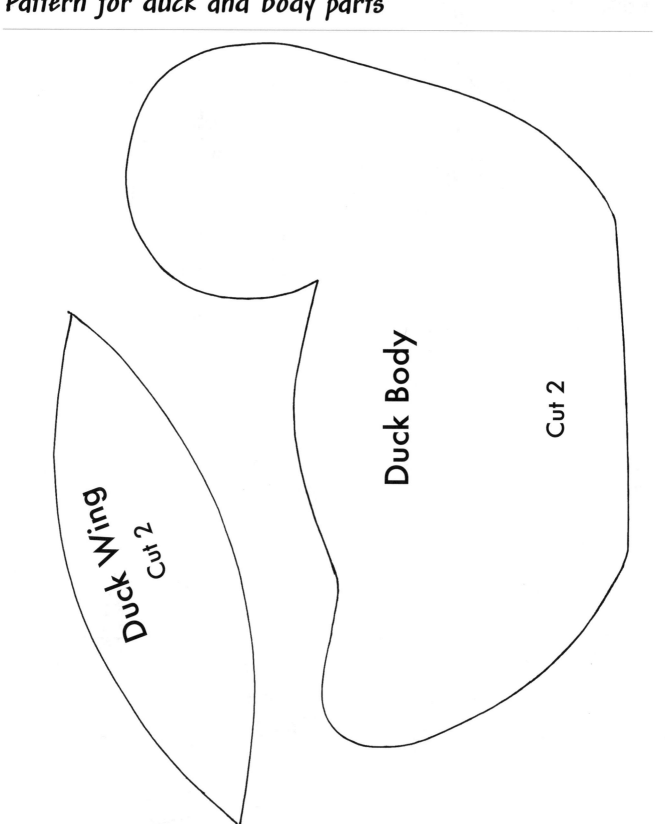

Duck Body

Cut 2

Duck Wing Cut 2

Pattern for turtle parts

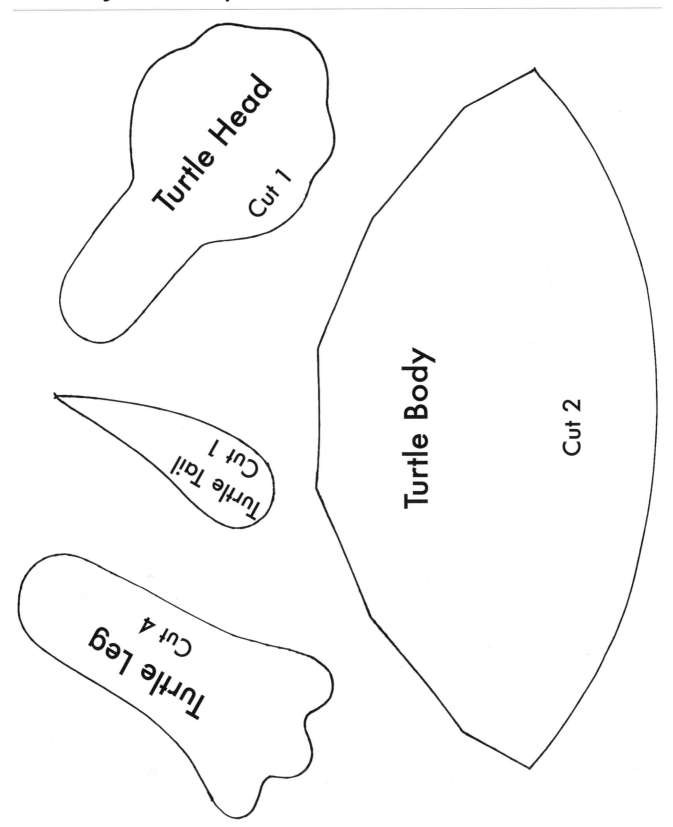

Turtle Head
Cut 1

Turtle Tail
Cut 1

Turtle Body
Cut 2

Turtle Leg
Cut 4

Pattern for beaver and duck parts

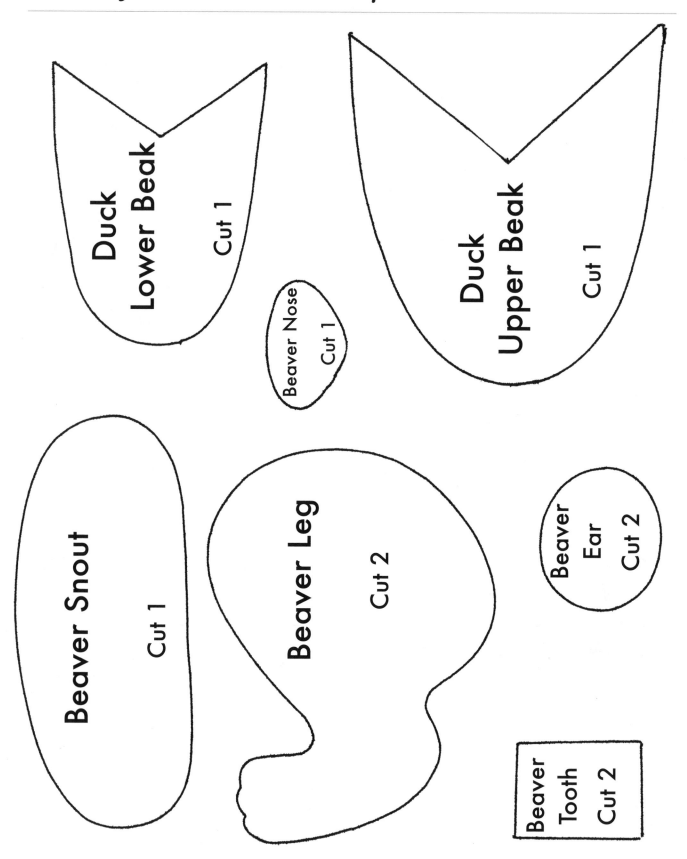

Duck
Lower Beak

Cut 1

Beaver Nose

Cut 1

Duck
Upper Beak

Cut 1

Beaver Snout

Cut 1

Beaver Leg

Cut 2

Beaver
Ear
Cut 2

Beaver
Tooth
Cut 2

Pattern for beaver body, tail, and arm

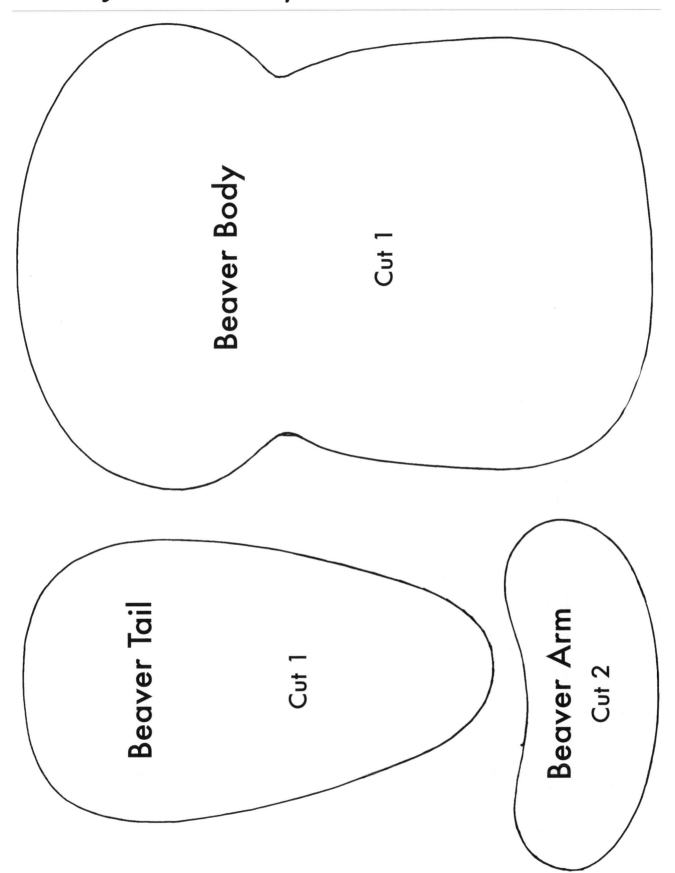

Beaver Body

Cut 1

Beaver Tail

Cut 1

Beaver Arm

Cut 2

Pattern for frog parts

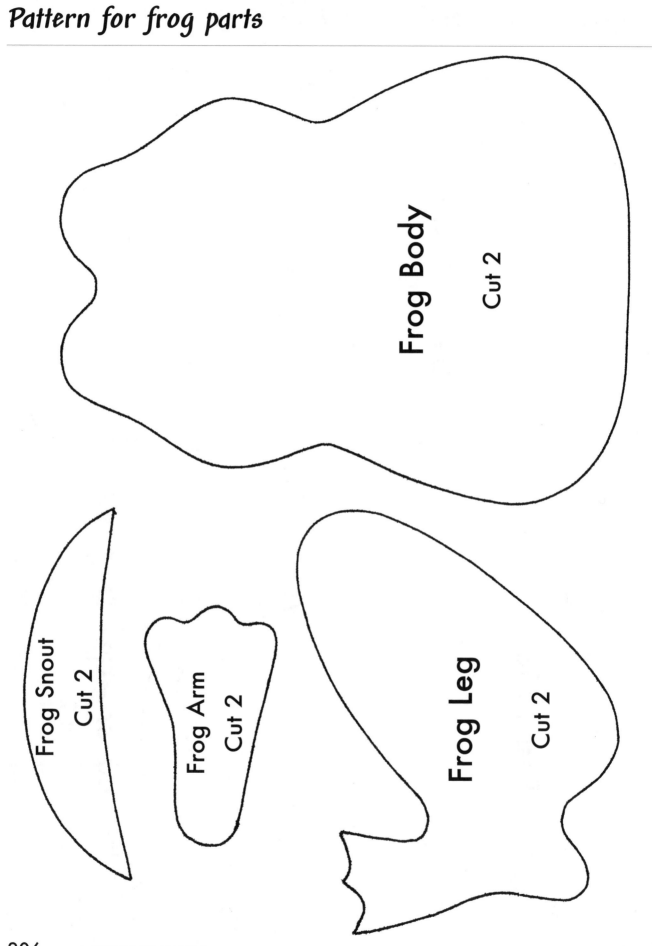

Frog Body

Cut 2

Frog Snout

Cut 2

Frog Arm

Cut 2

Frog Leg

Cut 2

Pattern for shark tail and teeth

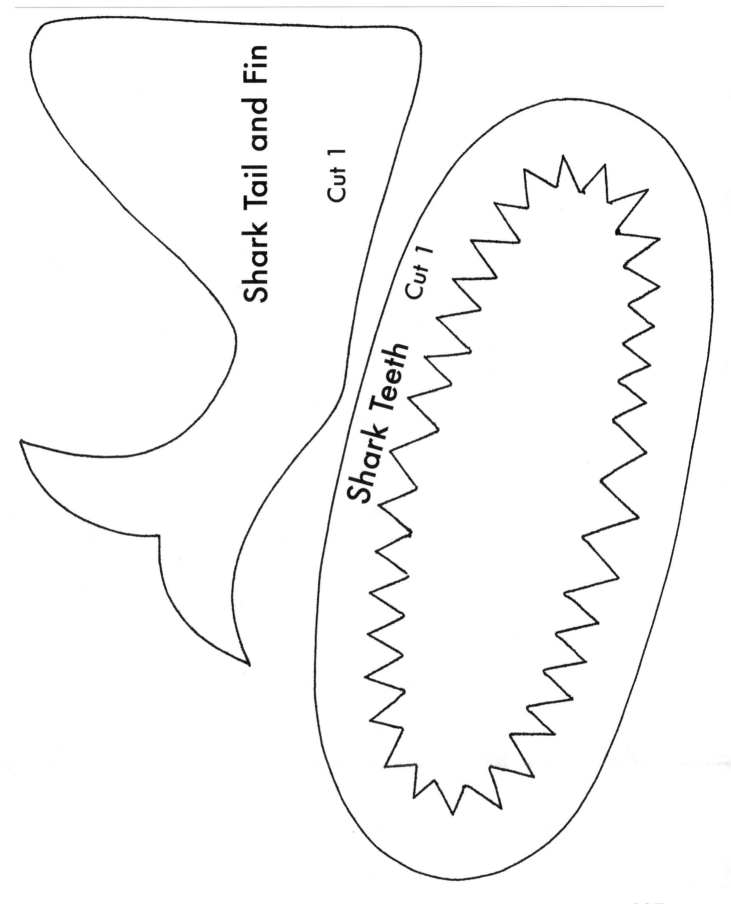

Shark Tail and Fin

Cut 1

Shark Teeth

Cut 1

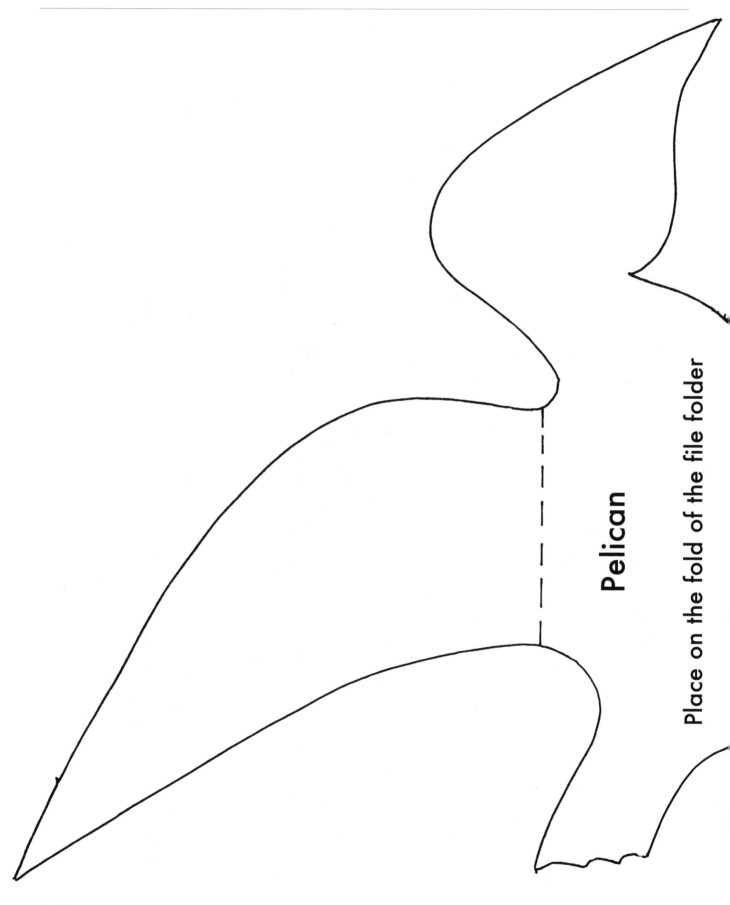

Pelican

Place on the fold of the file folder

Pattern for baby pterodactyl

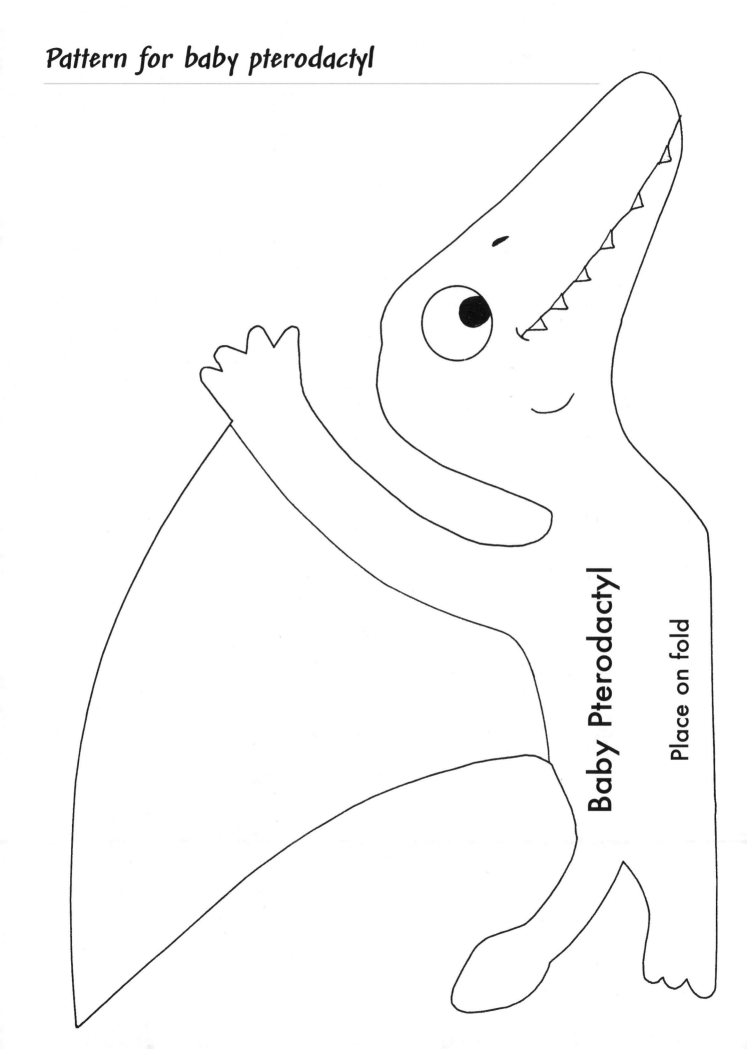

Baby Pterodactyl

Place on fold

Pattern 1 for mother pterodactyl

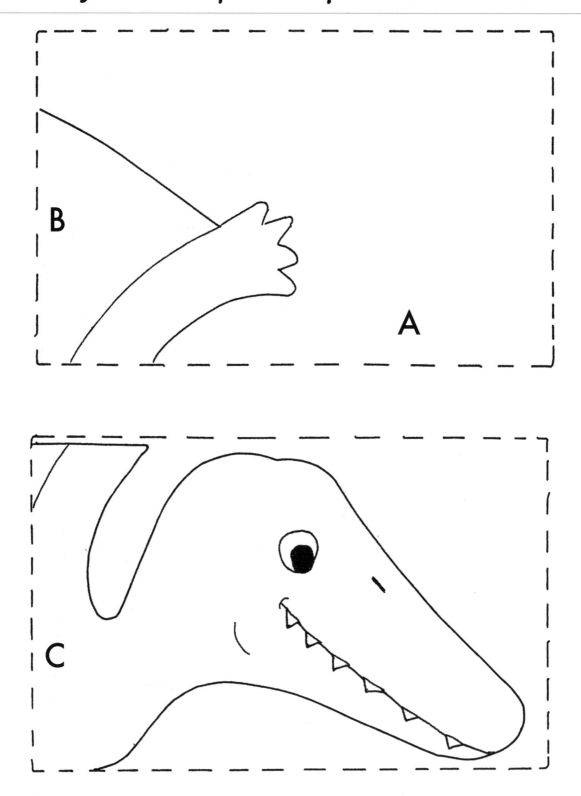

Pattern 2 for mother pterodactyl

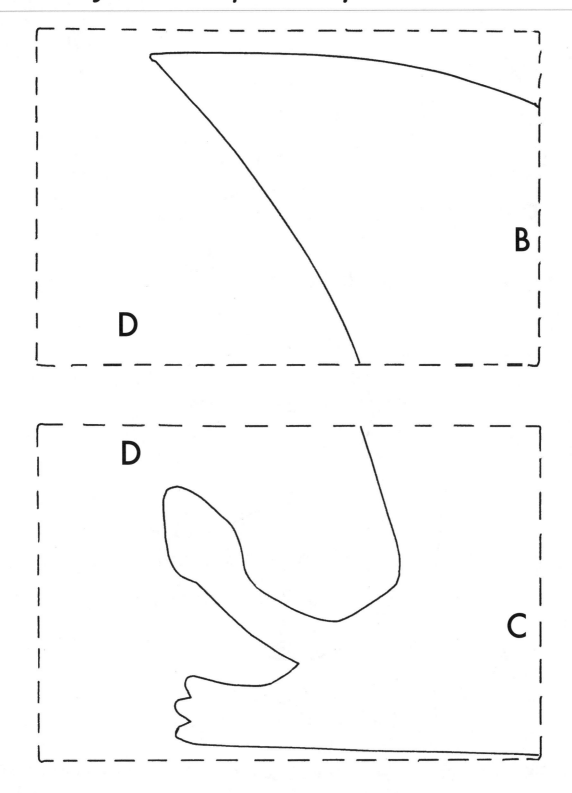

Pattern 1 for dog

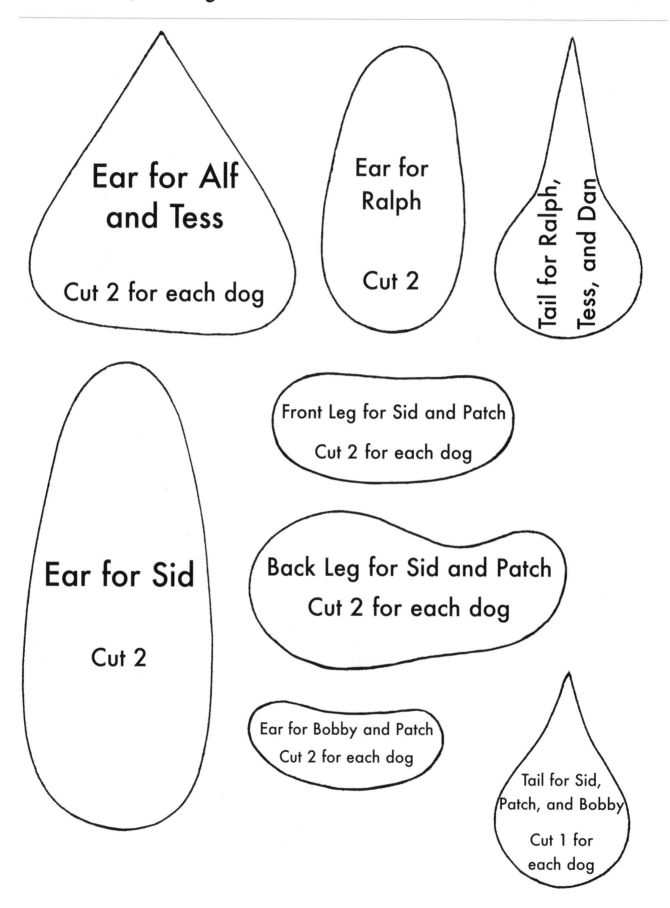

Ear for Alf and Tess

Cut 2 for each dog

Ear for Ralph

Cut 2

Tail for Ralph, Tess, and Dan

Ear for Sid

Cut 2

Front Leg for Sid and Patch

Cut 2 for each dog

Back Leg for Sid and Patch
Cut 2 for each dog

Ear for Bobby and Patch
Cut 2 for each dog

Tail for Sid, Patch, and Bobby

Cut 1 for each dog

Pattern 2 for dog

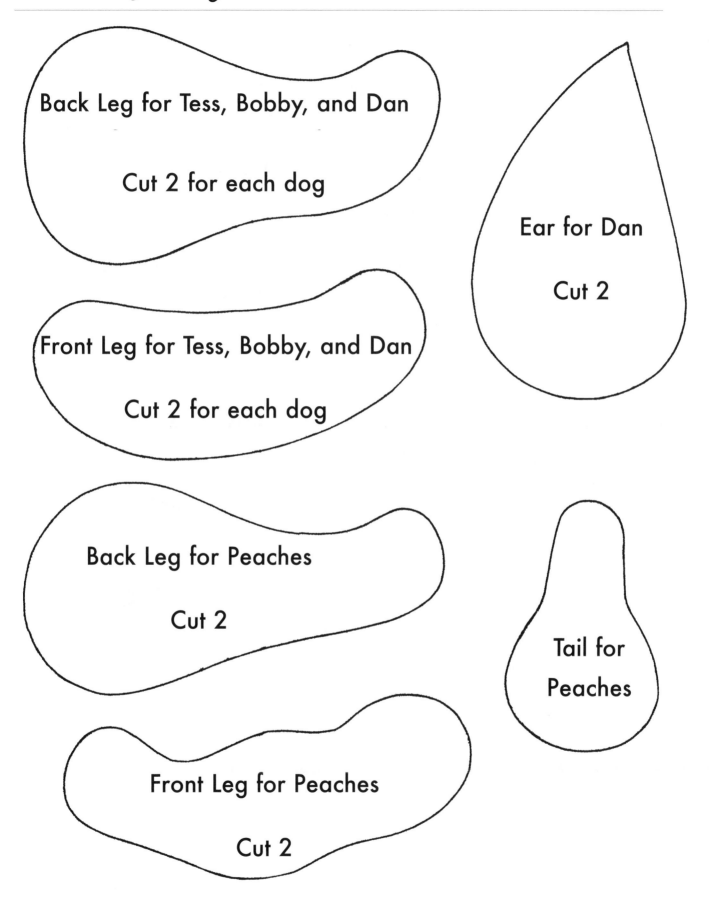

Back Leg for Tess, Bobby, and Dan

Cut 2 for each dog

Front Leg for Tess, Bobby, and Dan

Cut 2 for each dog

Ear for Dan

Cut 2

Back Leg for Peaches

Cut 2

Front Leg for Peaches

Cut 2

Tail for Peaches

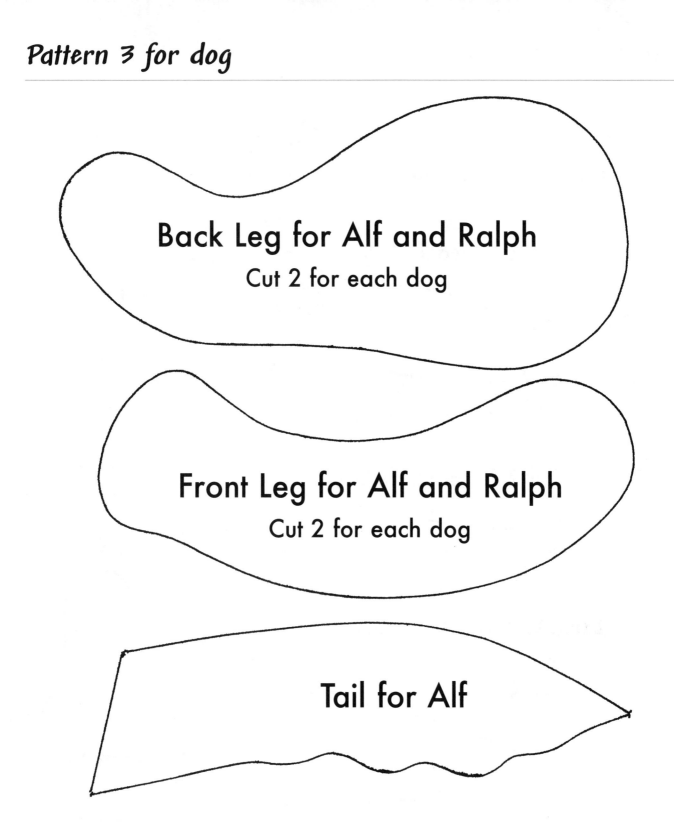

Back Leg for Alf and Ralph
Cut 2 for each dog

Front Leg for Alf and Ralph
Cut 2 for each dog

Tail for Alf

Pattern 4 for dog

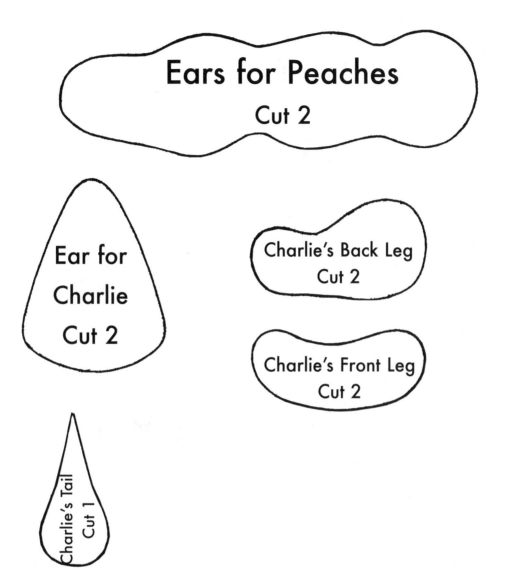

Ears for Peaches
Cut 2

Ear for
Charlie
Cut 2

Charlie's Back Leg
Cut 2

Charlie's Front Leg
Cut 2

Charlie's Tail
Cut 1

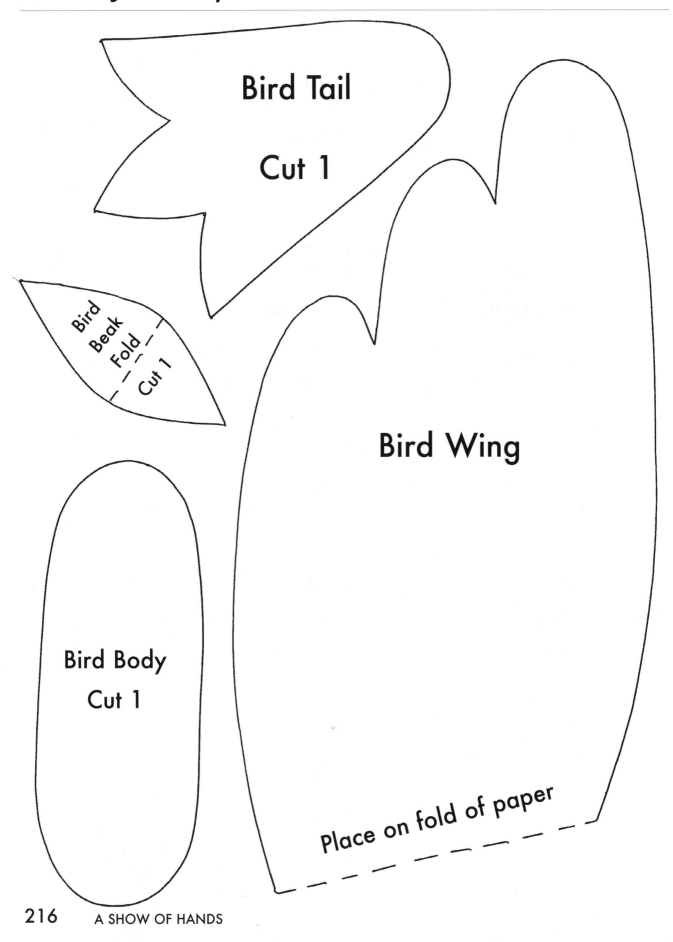

Bird Tail

Cut 1

Bird
Beak
Fold
Cut 1

Bird Wing

Bird Body

Cut 1

Place on fold of paper

Pattern for butterfly parts

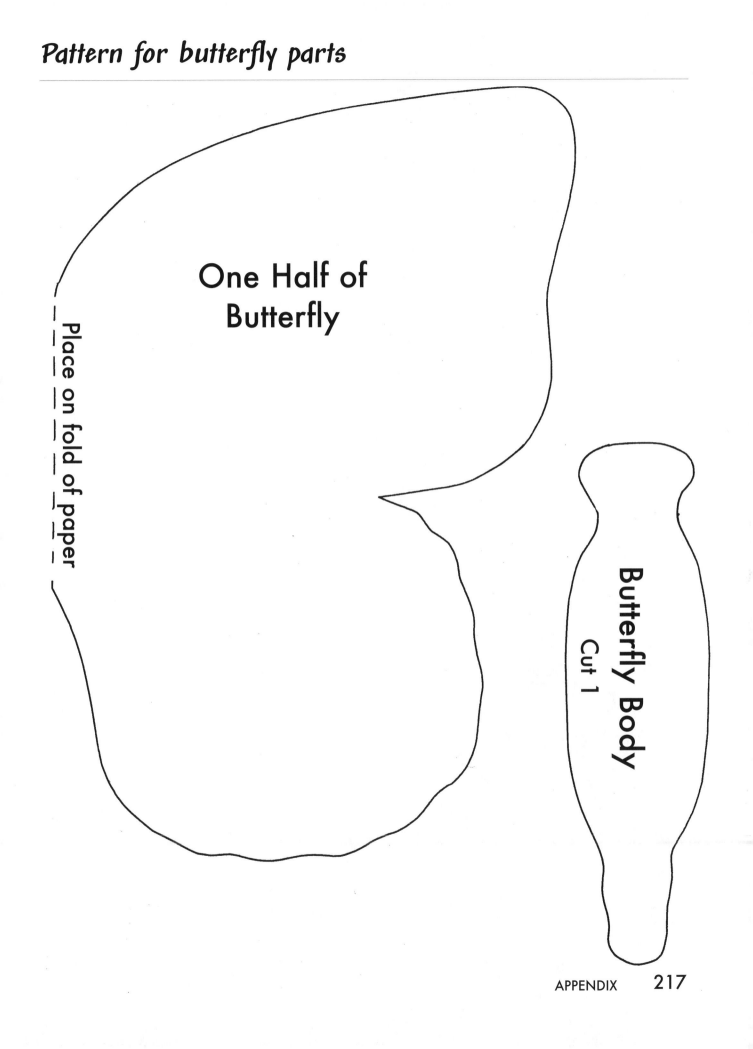

Place on fold of paper

One Half of
Butterfly

Butterfly Body
Cut 1

Glossary

CLOZE TECHNIQUE: An assessment technique that allows teachers to find out how much students know about a given topic. The teacher begins a phrase or sentence, and leaves a pregnant pause before ending. For example, "And then the big bad wolf said, 'Little pig, little pig, let me in,' and the piggy said . . ." In this example, most children would shout, "Not by the hair of my chinny-chin-chin!" verifying their knowledge of the story's sequence and content.

CREATE ATMOSPHERE: Allowing the children to create the atmosphere of the story by inviting them to imagine the attributes of the setting. For example, before doing an underwater story with puppets, the children are invited to splash water on their legs and faces, smell the salt air, feel the sun on their faces, listen to the seagulls, or describe a fish they see in the water. This may be done using mime and imagination, or it may be done using props like a box of sand, a spray bottle, a parachute, or an environmental sounds tape. This technique allows the children to get into the "mood" of the story.

EXPOSED PUPPETRY: Using puppets without a stage.

INVITATION TO PRETEND: Asking the children to do a few simple movements and lines with a puppet before beginning the activity. An invitation to pretend allows the children to enter the role of puppeteer gradually so that when they become more involved they are less likely to be shy and more likely to understand the concept.

ORACY: Pertaining to oral language skills. Oracy complements literacy to make up communication skills. The term "oracy" as compared to "oral" also references the bridge between spoken communication and written communication. This connection or overlapping is crucial for young children with emerging communication skills.

PICTURE WALK: Going through a book page by page with the children while telling the story rather than reading it. The teacher may include a discussion of the pictures, asking the children to interpret them as they go on their "walk." This technique can be used with books that are aimed at a slightly older age group but have value for young children.

PUPPET CHARACTERS: The four kinds of puppet characters are people, animals, inanimate objects, and fantasy characters.

PUPPET PLEDGE: A pledge that children and their puppets recite to reinforce appropriate puppet use.

PUPPET TYPES: Puppet types are defined by how puppets are operated. They include finger, hand, rod, shadow, marionette or string, object puppets, and hat puppets.

PUPPET USES: Classroom puppets are divided into two categories: puppets primarily manipulated by the teacher and puppets used by the children. Types of teacher-manipulated puppets include teacher assistant, task assistant, student, specialty, and reward puppets. Puppets used by children include puppet show, creative play, and student task puppets.

STORYTELLING STYLE OR TABLETOP PUPPETRY: All of the puppets, scenery, and props are sitting on the tabletop in full view of the audience throughout the narrative. The puppeteer simply manipulates the items as they are referenced in the story.

Resources

Professional Development

Bredekamp, Sue, and Carol Copple, eds. 1997. *Developmentally appropriate practice in early childhood programs serving children from birth through age eight.* Washington, D.C.: NAEYC.

Brown, Victoria, and Sarah Pleydell. 1999. *The dramatic difference: Drama in the preschool and kindergarten classroom.* Portsmouth, N.H.: Heinemann.

Gardner, Howard. 1993. *Frames of mind: The theory of multiple intelligences.* New York: Basic Books.

———. 1999. *Intelligence reframed.* New York: Basic Books.

Henson, Cheryl, and the Muppet Workshop. 1994. *The Muppets make puppets! Book and puppet kit: How to make puppets out of all kinds of stuff around your house.* New York: Workman.

Katz, Lilian. 1993. Dispositions as educational goals. *ERIC/EECE Publications Catalog* ED 363454.

Morrison, George S. 1998. *Early childhood education today.* Upper Saddle River, N.J.: Prentice-Hall, Inc.

Piaget, Jean. 1977. *The origins of intelligence in children.* New York: International Universities Press, Inc.

Wisniewski, David, and Donna Wisniewski. 1997. *Worlds of shadow: Teaching with shadow puppetry.* Englewood, Colo.: Teacher Ideas Press.

Word, Cynthia. Dancing through the day: Professional development workshop. Offered through Wolf Trap Institute for Early Learning Through the Arts in Vienna, Va.

Additional books and materials on puppetry in education are available through The Puppeteers of America Inc., 26 Howard Ave., New Haven, Conn. 06519-2809

Picture Books

Bang, Molly. 1983. *Ten, nine, eight.* New York: Greenwillow.

Bunting, Eve. 1997. *Ducky.* New York: Clarion Books.

Carle, Eric. 1987. *A house for Hermit Crab.* Natick, Mass.: Picture Book Studio.

———. 1999. *The very clumsy click beetle.* New York: Philomel Books.

Clements, Andrew. 1988. *Big Al*. Saxonville, Mass.: Picture Book Studio.

Ets, Marie Hall. 1963. *Gilberto and the wind*. New York: Viking Children's Books.

Flack, Marjorie. 1932. *Ask Mr. Bear*. New York: Macmillan Books for Young Readers.

Fleming, Denise. 1993. *In a small, small pond*. New York: Henry Holt & Company.

Gibbie, Mike. 2000. *Small Brown Dog's bad remembering day*. New York: Dutton Children's Books.

Ginsburg, Mirra. 1974. *Mushroom in the rain*. New York: Macmillan Books for Young Readers.

Kalan, Robert. 1995. *Jump, Frog, jump*. New York: William Morrow.

Packard, Mary. 1997. *I am not a dinosaur*. New York: Scholastic.

Pfister, Marc. 1992. *The rainbow fish*. New York: North-South Books.

Tolstoy, Aleksei Nikolayevich. 1999. *The gigantic turnip*. Cambridge, Mass.: Barefoot Books.